Learning About Dogs

MW00804734

Learning Games

Kay Laurence

Printed in the U.S. and distributed by
Karen Pryor ClickerTraining and Sunshine Books
49 River Street, Waltham, MA 02453
www.clickertraining.com
Sales: U.S. Toll Free 800-472-5425
        781-398-0754

First published in 2007

Learning About Dogs Limited

PO Box 13, Chipping Campden, Glos, GL55 6WX. UK

Copyright © 2007 Kay Laurence

All rights reserved worldwide. No part of this publication may be reproduced,
stored in a retrieval system, or transmitted, in any form or by any means,
electronic, mechanical, photocopying, recording or otherwise, without prior
permission of the publisher and copyright holder.

Kay Laurence has asserted the moral right to be identified as the author of
this work

ISBN 978-1-890-94836-8

Books in the Clicker Trainers Course series by Kay Laurence:

Clicker Foundation Trainer Level 1

Clicker Novice Trainer Level 2

Clicker Intermediate Trainer Level 3

Books for specialised interests to progress from Level 2

Clicker World Competition Obedience

Clicker Dances with Dogs

Clicker Agility for Fun and Fitness by Diana Bird

Clicker Gundog by Helen Phillips

Click for Grooming by Karen McCarthy

Teaching Dogs Magazine for up-to-date news on clicker training

www.clickertraining.com

CONTENTS

INTRODUCTION

Learning Games is a collection of interactive training exercises that pull together many different aspects of teaching and learning.

Over the last 7 years I have travelled around the world meeting hundreds of clicker trainers and their dogs. This "second generation" of trainers are developing dogs with tremendous skills and learning capacity. They are exceeding the expectations of the early clicker trainers and beginning to outgrow established methods.

What makes them so talented? How are they developing these superior skills? Teaching skills are improving all the time and more importantly, the teaching style has removed the stress load for the learner.

They can remember what they have learned over several years. They develop simple skills into amazingly complex movements. They have repertoires exceeding 100 behaviours on cue. These are mostly average dogs, living in the average household with a dog-friendly lifestyle. Not with professional dog trainers, but someone who is passionate about their dogs, enjoys interactive learning and finds teaching their dog highly reinforcing. Our communication with the dogs has developed into an exquisite language boosted by our mutual passion for learning and understanding each other.

Now we can take a look at how these dogs have become super-learners. A curriculum of specific collections of exercises can develop our youngsters, or take a damaged dog and re-build them.

The final behaviour often drives our teaching agenda. We want heelwork, we want a paw wave, we want a clean jump. That single minded focus can overlook an integral element: there is a learning process that is impacting on the dog's brain development and cognitive skills. Heelwork teaches dogs physical movement and a high degree of self awareness in their relative location to you. A paw wave isolates a very specific movement to one part of their body. These underlying generic skills can be applied to new behaviours, and by learning heelwork and paw waves, other behaviours become easier to acquire.

Learning Games should always be fun for both you and the dog. This is not hilarious, roll on the floor fun, but challenging enough to keep you engaged, daring enough to excite, interactively rich, where both learner and teacher are enjoying the game. Play is nature's school room. Through play life skills are acquired. Survival and hunting techniques are developed and mental capacity is stretched. Bonding takes place between the participants. Your teaching sessions should all include these elements, you are really "playing" with your dog.

I hope you all have fun with the book, make a plan or dip in when you want some clicker time. I am very much looking forward to the third generation of super learners ... they are going to be some special kind of dogs and people.

Kay Laurence

My thanks for everyone who has contributed to my learning process, consciously or otherwise. In particular the fabulous Team Genabacab and the Bark Less Wagging More Learners.

1 How to Use the Book

GAMES

All Games will develop your dog, but some Games are excellent at developing specific skills. Perhaps when you start with one Game you will realise your dog needs the opportunity to develop skills with a complimentary game.

The Games are not laid out in any specific order to follow, but collected with common techniques explained in the first section.

CHAPTER 3: GAMES WITH OBJECTS covers all the different behaviours that can be taught with targeting. An extensive language builds up with many different objects cueing different parts of the dog or different actions with the whole of the dog.

CHAPTER 4: GAMES MOVEMENTS takes a close look at developing fitness, from every day movements, movements for older dogs, developing youngsters and specialised sports dogs.

CHAPTER 5: GAMES WITH THE SAUSAGE food is reward, food is also prey. Learning the play games with food livens the plainest of training sessions.

CHAPTER 6: GAMES FROM THE DOG is a collection of dog originated actions. The ideas come from within the dog, demonstrate what they like to do and give us access to the cool behaviours that amaze non-clicker folk.

CHAPTER 7: GAMES FOR SELF CONTROL put the fun back into growing up. Self control needs regular and specific practice. These games make the learning easier and the time invested richer.

CHAPTER 8: GAMES PUZZLES is the double "wow" section. Things you did not know dogs could learn, and learn easily. Probably the chapter to blow you out of your chair, but also make you think.

In each game there is:

OUTLINE of the learning process and objectives.

LEVEL of teacher / learner skill recommended:

1 - beginner teacher

2 - some previous teaching experience and training skills required

3 - precision shaping with good observation and timing skills. A dog with experience of free shaping and with an ability to work through puzzles.

PREVIOUS SKILLS that either you or the dog will need.

RESOURCES above and beyond your optimum learning environment, and basic tools of clicker and treats.

PATTERN OF PROGRESS takes you step by step through the criteria that will achieve the final behaviour.

CLICK to mark. This may change with the criteria. Ensure you understand what you are trying to click, before you try to click.

REWARD location. This may also change with the learning and is critical in ensuring the optimum learning environment. What, where, how and when you deliver the reward is as important as what you click.

A second page for each Game gives additional variations that can be developed. Many Games are the foundation behaviours for more complex behaviours.

At the end:

GLOSSARY contains all the jargon that clicker training seems to nurture. We often develop terms in our own use that become the jargon of the future.

INDEX OF GAMES is a list of all the games for quick reference.

CHAPTER 2: TEACHING TECHNIQUES

This chapter should be read by everyone before they collect their clicker. It covers the techniques that the Games will assume you are familiar with.

Much of the established methods of clicker training originated with captive animals or from people interested in developing the clicker training science. These techniques are not necessarily appropriate for dog-owner trainers who share their lives and homes with their dogs.

At Learning About Dogs we have developed some techniques that have a deep impact on the capacity of the learner. These techniques may be a change from your existing knowledge of clicker training, but please, read them through, try out the techniques on one or two games before you assess their value in your training programme.

My agenda begins with the dogs and I use clicker training to explore my dogs' potential and personalities. At the same time we enjoy exceptionally rich quality time together in the process. This colours my approach to selecting and developing training techniques that are as dog friendly as possible. In many instances it may take longer since I avoid adding pressure to the dog, causing unnecessary frustration or betraying the teacher-learner trust.

As keen as you are to get started, you are NOT going to teach a single dog everything in the book.

No previous experience is needed, but the clicker training books for Foundation and Novice Trainers would provide a very good basis.

DEVELOPING YOUR DOG

Most dogs will develop to healthy, active individuals given a rich, dog-friendly growing environment. Our living style with dogs is becoming rather less dog friendly. We often have single dogs, limited opportunities for normal dog behaviour, and added pressure from society to compromise our dog's well being through unnatural restrictions. They cannot learn through chasing, protection, guarding, noisy play, wrestling etc., which can impact on their mental and physical development.

Finding the balance for your dog depends on your ability to assess their level of contentment. Stress caused by our lifestyles may not be a factor we can change, but through developing our dog's cognitive capacity, building an ability to adapt and change and puzzle through a variety of solutions we can promote a dog more able to adapt into urban life.

There is no reason why a healthy dog should not thoroughly enjoy a busy urban life. A routine of fairly inactive weekdays with highly active weekends is a good ratio. Even Border Collies on a sheep farm only work hard in seasonal cycles, and many learn to "hang out" around the yard keeping themselves entertained or waiting for human activity. My dogs have pretty good access to deciding what to do with their days. The youngsters play in the early morning, early evening, feed late in the day and sleep a lot in between. Evenings are often spent indoors in warmth and comfort watching TV. Access to me is variable, training time with me likewise and the same with walks up the hill. The routine is not the same from one day to the next and changes with the weather (I am a fair weather walker).

I believe they are content. They live as a group, averaging 7 dogs of two breeds: Gordon Setters and Border Collies. They have an age range over 12 years and no particular inter-dog anxieties. They chill together, tease each other, eat at a mutual distance, compete to get through the doorways and are disappointed when left behind. Right now I am working upstairs on the computer and I can see them lying with a view of the front door, close together watching Gloucestershire clouds travel past. Mabel, the senior queen, is lying behind my chair, waiting for me to roll over her tail. She finds the excitement of the youngsters too over stimulating for her age, and takes compulsory morning naps.

Other factors, such as a healthy diet combined with a good lifestyle results in rare veterinary visits.

But with our busy lifestyles we do not always have as much time as we would wish for to spend with our dogs. It becomes more important that the time we have is good quality for both us and the dogs. Going for a walk may contribute to our physical well being, but often does not enhance our relationship. The dogs are very often involved in their own agenda, as are we, and shared pleasures may not be obvious. I may take an interest in wild life, but not in wearing the local badger's toilet. Equally the dogs have little interest in what trees are blooming, dying or have fallen over.

Personally the time I truly connect with the dogs as individuals is when grooming and training, and the odd visits on the sofa or passing on the stairs. The particular stresses my dogs have to contend with are development as an individual and a personal relationship with me.

For each dog I look to balance mental and physical development, as a healthy adult canine and for my particular interests.

COGNITIVE (MENTAL) DEVELOPMENT

Your dog's mental capacity, speed of thinking and lateral thinking will develop through learning. As puppies their brains are designed to develop different skills at different periods. New neural pathways connecting more parts of the brain are laid down as their learning makes demands on more storage space and routing systems. Their brains will go on developing if the demand is maintained. Learning is not restricted to the young, it is a lifeskill, a muscle that needs to be exercised, pushed, opposed, strengthened and used regularly.

With regular teaching sessions we can ensure excellent mental development and a mutually enjoyable time. Learning will not be restricted to just the dogs either, they will teach us as much as we think we are teaching them.

They develop:

AWARENESS of the click and the absence of the click. The awareness that they control the outcome and your reactions.

ABILITY TO ANALYSE themselves. What happened that caused the click, how to repeat it. This involves memory development. Could it be where the dog is or an action that it is are doing? This encourages lateral thinking.

MENTAL STAMINA, to work for solutions, to try harder and to be able to work for longer periods.

CONCENTRATION against distractions and collating information from experience. They learn to focus and ignore distracting stimuli.

PUZZLE SOLVING SKILLS that can be transferred to real life situations. Unfortunately, this is also a measure of self confidence, where lack of success is not emotionally depressing, but just information that drives the dog to try harder.

CREATIVITY and an ability to entertain us, suggest behaviours that we may like to reinforce. Creative dogs used to be known as naughty dogs.

MEMORY SKILLS of what works, what doesn't work. Remembering the cues for over 100 different behaviours, situations, routines and friends.

CONCEPTS AND ADVANCED THINKING. High level puzzle solving that brings many other skills together. Self confidence to explore and suggest solutions. Analyse opportunities for repetition.

ADAPTABILITY through a rich range of different learning experiences that demand mental gymnastics. This enhances their coping mechanism and ability to adapt to stress.

INNER CONFIDENCE through experiential learning success. A confident (normal) dog will not fear failure and keep striving for success. Conversely the process of striving for success builds confidence in the learner.

Most importantly they maintain a desire to learn, an inquisitive mind that enjoys new situations and never hesitates when opportunities arrive. (Hmm ... not worn that badger poo before!)

PHYSICAL SKILLS

Physical skills can be divided into:

ESSENTIAL LIFESKILLS for everyday life, inter communication and well being

SPECIFIC SKILLS for sports (agility, freestyle, field work, heelwork etc) to maintain fitness and be injury free.

LIFE SKILLS

BALANCE DEVELOPMENT, for greeting without pushing or knocking over people, waving a paw when standing, cocking a leg.

MOVEMENTS to sit, down, rollover, with ease and as reflex actions, reaching that scratch, self grooming. Learn to relax, fold into beds, settle and contain excitement. Rolling upsidedown after food, stretching when waking.

FAMILIARITY with range of environmental situations. New surfaces, how to react, find balance and movement, travel in cars, keep balance, relax, walk over bridges and meet technology.

JUMP onto and off surfaces, grooming tables, up and down stairs cases, steps, sofas and beds.

PLAY games, wrestling, retrieve, jumping, catching, chasing, digging, burying.

INTER-COMMUNICATION. Talk dog: use of balance, poise, relaxed ease, tail movement. Subtleties of stature, facial movements, building of confidence, reducing tension. Balancing to cock a leg with the right attitude.

SPORTS SKILLS

ACCELERATION for movement or jumping, over some distance or from standing.

CHANGE OF MOMENTUM, collecting their energy or expelling the energy in bursts.

BALANCE in turning and maintaining a balance, speed and spatial awareness, when to come out of turn and how to tighten the turn.

JOINT extension and flexibility. Maintaining supple joints that are injury free,

MUSCLE STRENGTH for endurance, maintenance of movements, finer movement control.

PHYSICAL STAMINA aerobic development that ensures good blood supply to all requirements of the working body.

RESTING, and semi resting. Repairing after exercise and warm up for high activity.

2 Teaching Skills

Learning is a three way interaction:

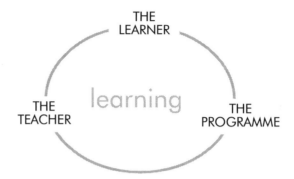

If learning is making slow progress, or becoming too complex to acquire, then all three elements need to be examined for improvement. In my experience it is very rarely the learner that needs improvement, it is the teacher or the programme that needs to be changed.

Throughout the book I have carefully described how progress can be made to achieve the outcome of the Game. We must allow the same detailed development of our own skills and ensure that our element of the learning interaction is the very best it can be.

OPTIMUM LEARNING ENVIRONMENT

This must be the ideal place to teach the particular Game. It may be your kitchen, your garden or a special training area.

Check:

 ◆ the work surface gives the dog confidence, when food is thrown it can easily be seen.

 ◆ there are minimal distractions from other dogs, scents, people, technology (no telephones!) etc.

 ◆ the dog is comfortable in this area, able to settle down and when training is completed relaxes quickly

 ◆ you are comfortable in the area, have a good chair, place to write notes, place to read from your Learning Games book

 ◆ any equipment needed is ready close to hand

◆ the time of day may be varied, but suits both you and the dog for energy levels.

◆ the "do not disturb" sign has been placed on the door

If you have anxieties about learning at any time in your past history, it is very rarely the subject that is at fault, but the teacher, or the programme that the teacher had to work within. You cannot "hate" maths. If it is taught to you at your learning pace with passion and motivation you can learn and enjoy it at the same time. Most learning is turned sour by the speed of the teaching forcing the learner to over reach themselves and thereby fail. A dog cannot "hate" obedience or "hate" repetition. It becomes the responsibility of the teacher to continually analyse progress, make change to the program or their teaching style. At every stage, as the teacher, you must seek evidence that the dog is comfortable in its learning and what it is learning is what you think you are teaching.

When you watch great teachers, of any subject or any type of pupil, they will have common skills in place. Some of these are innate and some are acquired through experience and practice:

TIMING SKILLS: an ability to observe that the correct action is about to take place and the click is on the mark. Movement of actions, the speed of the reward and the pace of the lesson, all suit the learner's speed.

COMMUNICATION: great teachers speak the language of their pupil. At their speed, with clarity and continually checking understanding. They avoid presumptions made about prior knowledge, they draw the best from their learners.

SETTING UP THE LEARNING: an ability to ensure that the learner is curious, motivated and easily acquires the learning without stress. For the very sensitive learners: an errorless programme. For the strong learners: room to explore and to experience the correct proportion of failure and success.

SHAPING PLANS: a clear idea of how the learning may progress. Whether the outcome or the process is the key objective.

PATIENCE IS KNOWLEDGE DISGUISED: yup. When your patience is wearing thin, remind yourself of this. Observing your super-learner (a dog) go through their puzzling, is a very precious and privileged moment, to be savoured and enjoyed.

REINFORCERS AND ALTERNATE REWARDS: rewards need to be planned to compliment the learning and the achievement. They need to be varied, stimulating and interesting.

ENJOY THE TEACHING PROCESS: learning to have fun in your lesson is critical. Dogs are fun animals. They are naughty, cheeky, testing, creative, inquisitive and make us smile without telling jokes.

CREATIVITY: keeping the lessons full of imaginative ideas, new objects, new places, crazy cues.

ORGANISED LESSONS: keep records of what you are teaching, progress made, analyse areas in need of extra time, assess yourself, your learner, your programme and continually plan your forward progress.

WHAT IS TODAY'S LESSON?

Before I begin teaching the dog I am very clear what I hope to achieve over the next few minutes. The dog will know within seconds what my plan is, and trust me to guide them along their learning path. If I pick up the Whippit they will know instantly what Games we are playing. If I stock up with treats and toss a mat onto the floor they can respond straight away with a position on the mat.

If I sit in my chair facing the dog, place an object between us, they know we are free shaping, or learning something new that has no known cue. This is the only expected response to that learning environment. As soon as I make eye contact they begin exploring what it is I will click for. I inadvertently taught eye contact as a cue to begin, when trying to count out treats, take data and swap objects during the sessions. The dogs were constantly trying something before I was ready, or didn't have the clicker. So I purposefully ignored anything I could see from the corner of my eye, until I was fully "ready to go". The dogs picked up this cue extremely quickly. In fact I can bumble around, setting up the chair, choosing objects, placing the treat box by the chair, doodling with the clicker, all taking a couple of minutes and by the time I am ready to go the dogs are diving into their learning. They follow the routine and you can see the anticipation build up.

Most Games will begin from this free shape opening position unless stated otherwise. Check:

◆ Optimum learning environment

◆ At least 100 treats ready to go

◆ The clicker

◆ Any shaping objects or equipment

MICRO SHAPE OR SHAPE BY ERROR REDUCTION?

You need to decide at which end of the "errorless" learning scale you will set up for the dog. At one end you have a sensitive learner, who needs absolutely NO errors during their learning. One hundred percent success from everything they try. This builds self confidence, desire to explore, try new things. Excellent for inhibited or learning damaged dogs.

At the other end we have a strong, fast learner with oodles of experience. They tend to rush in and "know" just what to do with that object, get a little over confident. Some degree of deliberate failure can focus this learner.

For all learners too much error, or no clicks, is depressing and will inhibit experimentation and creativity. All dogs will need a varying degree success throughout their learning from day to day and from exercise to exercise.

Micro shaping allows you to teach very refined behaviours with accuracy. But perhaps in this lesson you want your dog to memorise the incorrect behaviours as they progress, and ensure they avoid them. This may be particularly useful where the incorrect behaviours are very close to the correct behaviour. With errorless learning the dog only has knowledge of one way of doing the behaviour. Should the undesired behaviour happen by accident, they do not know not to avoid it. Sometimes you will need to give the confident learner the experience of failure, which is just information to a clicker dog, no emotional fallout, so that they can be more secure in the behaviour that is correct.

MICRO SHAPING little or no room for error		PLANNED ERRORS for extra focus on success
	MOST DOGS WILL LEARN IN THIS AREA	
Placement of reward is such that success is highly probable		Placement of reward is such that success is likely but not probable

LURING

Luring tends to have bad press. To dismiss luring is rather similar to dismissing demonstration. In many instances it is an entirely appropriate form of explanation to the dog. It can give a clear picture, show the outcome, demonstrate timing, pace, placement of the cues, targets or rewards. It gives us time to observe what the final behaviour will look like. The dog has not "learned" the behaviour, they have just followed their nose. We have no idea whether the dog is assessing what they are doing or just fixating on that piece of food as if it is the last food for a week.

Without the lure the behaviour is unlikely to happen, but the dog has just demonstrated how they can perform the behaviour at this moment in time. You may see some hesitation,some unsureness, a need for extra movement training or some stuttering in key areas. It allows us to plan the teaching, it gives us a clear picture of the learning gap.

After the click you can use the lure to set the dog up in the optimum position to start the behaviour again. For the learner it gives them a break. It is not taxing following a piece of food, but it can also give them some feeling for the behaviour.

OPEN OR FREE SHAPING

This is learning with minimal direction from the teacher. The dog explores possibilities and finds their path. They own their own progress. They have made the decisions that lead to their success. Their brain has developed solutions that will be retained easily. What you have taught yourself you can always re-acquire.

Additionally we are not dogs. We do not know what it is like for another individual to learn algebra or how to write poetry, so how can we begin to know how a dog will learn? Open or Free shaping lets the dog teach itself.

TARGETING

Targets are free shaped in acquisition but become the basis for our language to the dogs. A target can specify:

A PART OF THE DOG'S BODY: nose, chin, front left paw, back right paw, whole body

AN ACTION: move to stand on this mat, follow this target with your nose, touch this button with your paw, hold this item in your mouth

Targets are visual cues that allow us to build more complex behaviours. They are the building tools for the clicker trainer, and may or may not be part of the final behaviours.

LURING, SHAPING OR TARGETING?

Deciding which route to take will depend on the learner's and your skills. Each set of games will give you ideas that make the learning easier through targets or luring or shaping, but you must be prepared to adapt to meet your dog's needs.

ADDING CUES

Through out the book the process for adding or changing cues will be the New Cue - Old Cue system.

Dogs are extremely skilled at learning routines, and have an uncanny ability to anticipate. I know you have a routine for leaving the house. You will go through several actions, maybe with reluctance or maybe with purpose. These styles of your actions are cues to the dog. Am I coming with you or staying behind? They will begin to watch for the first cue which says they are coming along. The type of clothing you put on, your shoes, the training bag, the dog lead and then the car keys. Dogs can recognise that certain types of shoes are only worn when you take them for a walk. They will go to the front door, get excited or start barking anticipating the trip. They were not born knowing the difference between posh shoes and walking shoes. They learn to observe your routines and at which point they split into good news and bad news. We use the same technique to add a cue to a behaviour.

The dog may have learned to beg by touching their nose to the end of a target stick. This becomes the Old Cue. The New Cue will be "Beg". The new cue is given, pause, then the target stick is used to stimulate the behaviour. This is repeated until you see the dog anticipating the presentation of the target stick.

As soon as they begin to respond to the New Cue, the Old Cue can be used to reinforce the idea after the behaviour has commenced and then it can be dropped.

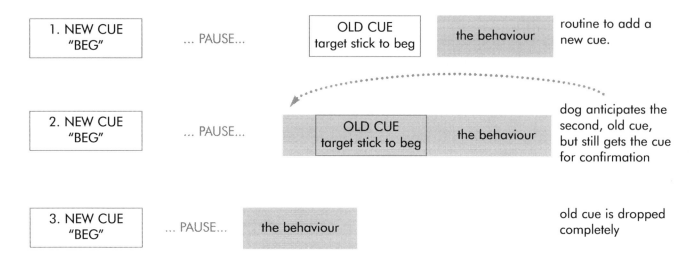

Your dog will become more skilled at transferring behaviours to the new cue as they get more experience and practice. The number of repetitions at each stage depends on the dog, the clarity of your cues and routine. You need to begin to see the signs of the dog anticipating the second, old cue, and give them room to show you what they think is happening. Nothing worse than someone asking you a question: "What was the name of the street where your school was?" And before you've had time to ponder, they jump in with the answer. Patience is knowledge disguised ... let the dog learn.

Inexperienced dogs may take 10–20 repetitions of step 1 and 2, and experienced dogs 3–5. Step 3 is practised many, many times on a regular basis to keep the connection fresh and easily accessed in the dog's memory.

STIMULUS / REACTION TO NEW CUE

Many times the behaviours we are seeking to acquire are stimulated by the dog's reaction to a stimulus. An example maybe the dog will look at sudden movement of an object on the end of a stick. We throw an object, run towards it and the dog will move with us. The dog is standing at a short distance and we throw their toy or piece of food behind them. As we raise our hand to throw, the dog will not continue moving towards us, but anticipate the thrown toy and hold their position, or move backwards.

Behaviours that are stimulated by our behaviours or situations trigger a reaction, very often an instinctive reaction. New cues can be attached to this in exactly the same way as the New Cue Old Cue protocol.

For hundreds of years sheepdogs have learned to turn left, turn right, stop, walk forward, and leave the sheep in exactly this process. The dog will be standing looking at standing sheep. The trainer will gradually encourage the sheep to move one way, the collie will instinctively react to prevent that movement with a turn to the left or right. The trainer will then give their whistle for the left or right (new cue) followed by moving the sheep (old cue) in the appropriate direction.

ENSURING "NOT UNLESS CUED"

This key piece of your training will prevent your dog struggling through their whole repertoire of possible behaviours when they hear a cue.

Before you add a new cue, decide what behaviour your dog should do if:

1. they do not know what the cue is
2. they have not been given a cue

This behaviour is know as the default behaviour. For my freestyle dogs it is standing in front of me, when walking on lead it is standing by the side of me checking in, for working on the sheep it is hold your place. The situation cues the default behaviour.

Remember that holding a clicker and treats, or a hand to your training bag are also cues. In any of these situations click and reward the dog for the default behaviour. No obvious cue, just the environmental cues.

This builds tremendous confidence for the dog, that you give them a clear description of the behaviour that you expect them to do.

When you add the new cue, after several repetitions of Step 3 (opposite page), begin to insert the default behaviour, rotating around "no cue" and "blah blah" (a cue the dog could not possibly understand) in any order.

For the "blah blah" cues offer words with quite different pitch and syntax to the new cue. If the new cue is "turn" then offer: "cheese on toast", " sugar plum fairies" etc, gradually getting closer in similarity to the new cue: "timing", "temperature" etc.)

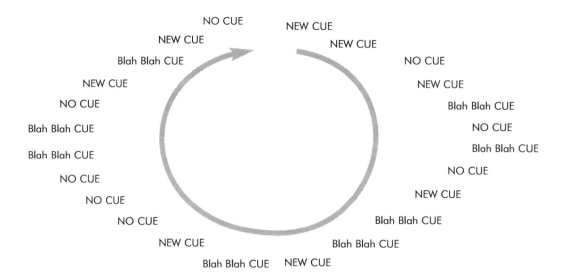

REWARD PATTERNS

The reward you use, how you deliver and where you deliver it will have more impact on the learning than the clicker. (I can hear you gasp.)

Regard the complete cycle of a behaviour:

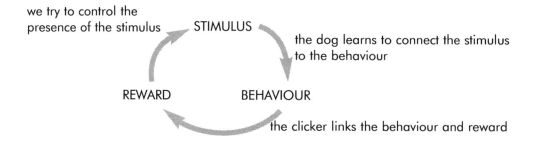

WHAT IS A REWARD?

Rewards come in many packages. You can only establish what is rewarding for your dog by the change in the behaviour. If it is rewarding it will maintain or get stronger, if not the behaviour will weaken or fade away. You must analyse three elements each time: What, How and Where. "When" is fixed in new learning, and is immediate. (The variable "When", will come into effect after the behaviour is well established and is dependent on the dog's experience, the number of behaviours in the chain etc.)

WHAT YOU DELIVER:

Food, a toy, physical contact, attention, eye contact or proximity? Make decisions about what value of reward needs to be delivered and what is emotionally appropriate: ie., do you want to build excitement or calmness?

HOW YOU DELIVER IT:

The style of delivery should enhance the learning. If you are looking for action then activity to collect the reward will compliment action in the subsequent behaviour. Quick movements of your hands and body will stimulate excitement, calm predicted movements will stimulate calmness and relaxed focus. The opposite strategy will also change the behaviour to increase the energy the dog is too slow, or decrease the energy when the dog is too fast.

In duration the reward and the behaviour need to be balanced

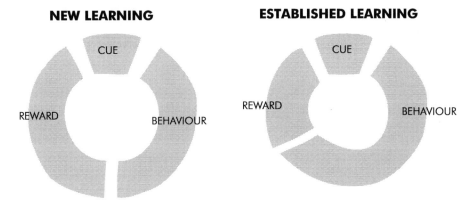

In energy, the reward and the behaviour need to be balanced

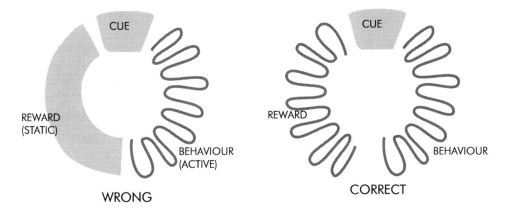

WHERE YOU DELIVER IT

If you are teaching the dog to remain stationary, calm and still, then the reward needs to be delivered to compliment that behaviour: for example learning to balance in the beg, the reward should be delivered direct to the dog when in the beg position, or if balance is not yet fluent, in the opening sit position.

If you are teaching a movement, for example walking backwards, delivering at a point where the dog can walk forward to collect will compliment the next behaviour of walking backwards. If you are teaching the dog to remain stationary, calm and still, then the reward needs to be delivered unhurried, and calmly.

Successfully combining all three elements make the subsequent behaviour easy for the dog to repeat.

For example: teaching a paw touch to an object:

> **WHAT** you deliver: small piece of averagely tasty food
>
> **HOW** you deliver it: calmly and with predictable movement
>
> **WHERE** you deliver it: off centering the dog over the front paw that is not going to make the action, encouraging their weight to remain on this leg.

For example: teaching a run to mat:

> **WHAT** you deliver: large piece of easy visible food, with some bounce
>
> **HOW** you deliver it: with speed and fast movements
>
> **WHERE** you deliver it: away from the target mat

REWARDS FOR OUTCOMES OR ACTIONS?

A behaviour that has no fixed start or end point is used for teaching a process. Once the process is achieved, polished and on cue, start and end points can be added. A target can be used to stimulate an action with its presence continuously cueing, or at the end of a behaviour that stimulates a direction or placement.

Lots of individual behaviours that teach the PROCESS of going around in a circle

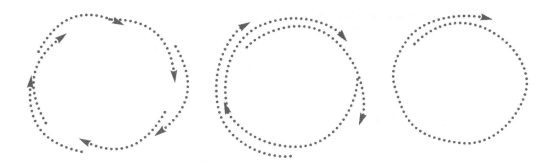

One behaviour, the OUTCOME, hitting the target, is generalised

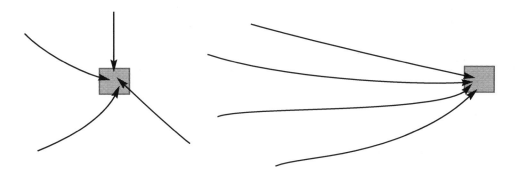

An outcome can be used to teach a process. If using targets as outcomes to stimulate an action to achieve that outcome, there will be a moment during training that the target will be faded and the action needs to remain. During the transfer to the final cue, a click will occur before the outcome is achieved. In the example of the "run ahead" behaviour, the cue "go" will trigger the run out action, which will be clicked. At that point the dog is very likely to turn to face you for reward.

Instead of using the clicker, use the cue for the mat as the click.

u   Set up the mat, refresh with several "to the mat" cues.

u   Give the new cue: "go"

u   As the dog responds to the "go" and begins the action, give the "to the mat" cue as the click. Click and reward on the mat as usual.

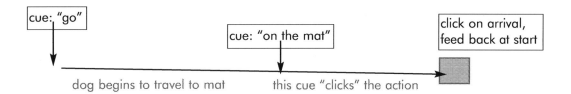

SAME LANGUAGE, DIFFERENT CLICKS

VISUAL CLICK

You can use a clicker for any behaviour especially if you think it will help the dog understand what you are trying to explain, but be wary of using the standard clicker close to the dog's ears. Equally, the springing open of the lure hand IS a visual click. It marks the moment when the dog can take the food—ie: what action (behaviour) has earned the reward.

FLICK CLICK

As the changing hand shape can indicate the action that has earned the reward, any movement of the arms can perform the same communication. Very often a movement towards the food pot or bag is a clear indication to the dog that they have:

   a) triggered that action some how, they have just sat, touched, moved etc.

   b) a reward usually follows

The clicker is more valuable than these visual clicks as the dog can work without the need to focus on our movements. But when our movements are part of the dog's focus, the visual clicks are extremely clear forms of communication.

CLICK FOR ACTION, FEED FOR RESTING

If you want to teach a sit position to heel that is followed by a speedy reaction to move off, then when shaping this behaviour, click for the action of sitting but always throw the food forwards for reward. This encourages the hip joints to retain tension during the sit. You can stimulate the opposite response by encouraging a settled sit of duration, by feeding in the sit. The muscles can then relax, and the position gets reinforcement, not the movement.

SO MANY THINGS TO LEARN!

Isn't it exciting? Enjoy the learning process rather than focus on the outcome and you will enjoy the journey. Look for Games that enhance your learning and develop your teaching skills as well as great fun for your dog.

3 GAMES with Objects

Target training is a wonderful teaching technique that simplifies learning for the dog and allows us to explore whole new areas of teaching.

For example. When I first began clicker training we started with two basic targets: the stick and the mat. I was satisfied with any type of interaction, variable duration and commitment. This generation of youngsters learn to target their nose to an object on the end of a stick. The object changes with different body parts. The behaviour changes with different actions. If the stick is stationary: touch the object, if the stick is moving: follow the object. I can now explain what I am trying to teach with much more clarity and understanding. How do I know this? This generation are incredibly skilled "targeteers". As they learn a new behaviour they seem to self assess the movement. Within a handful of repetitions they are demonstrating fluency. At this point I introduce the final cue, and they dismiss the need for the target almost immediately. They have generalised this learning strategy: let the target explain the behaviour, remember it, listen for the cue, anticipate the target, go off target.

Targeting adds strength to the final or performance cue. Previously I often acquired the same behaviours with luring or hand movements and needed to fade this as any hand movement become a distraction to finished behaviours. Many moves originated from hand movements and the dogs found them hard to ignore. The target never needs to be faded, as it is never present once the behaviour is transferred to a final cue, where as my hands and arms are always present and always talking, even if they are not moving, they are "talking".

In 2006 I was lucky enough to spend the day at the Shedd Aquarium in Chicago. Many thanks to Ken Ramirez I was able to observe a particularly effective use of a targets. In the dolphin pool there are approximately a dozen animals at any one time. A handful of trainers will go to the pool at regular times through the day. This is dictated by the animals' feeding schedule, which I surmised is similar to grazing throughout the day as opposed to single, or double, feed times we have with dogs.

At each training/feeding time opportunities for training or demonstrations are planned. One animal may need husbandry care, or fine tuning a specific behaviour for the display. The trainers each collect a bucket of fish containing a diet specific to the animal(s) they are feeding. Each trainer may have more than one or two animals to feed and train. Attached to the buckets are the "labels" for each animal. These are large plastic shapes in various colours and patterns: a star, a square, a flower, a paddle etc.

As the trainers arrive at pool side the dolphins begin to race around the edges. Each trainer will walk to a specific point on pool side, which is a reasonable spread around three sides. They co-ordinate the readiness and give the cue "come to station", at the same time they insert the plastic labels off the buckets, the targets, into the water. Each dolphin continues to race around until they find their "station". Each dolphin has their own target to indicate their feed and training station.

Ponder the application of that technique when training more than one dog at the same time? What if each dog has a separate target to indicate their nose-follow target? Each dog could have their own "station" target, possibly a mat or stool to wait on for their cues. Because dogs are more acute in their sight rather than hearing, their ability to recognise target shapes is great, therefore easier, than verbal cues.

WHAT ARE TARGETS?

A target is anything that cues a behaviour, it is technically an object stimulus.

The object can be a stimulus for: an action
                                           a specific body part
                                           a location

And also a combination of all these. The yellow star object was the cue for "station" for Remus, the action: maintain a vertical position and "at this location", was combined.

Careful planning will equip the dog with a range of target skills, that can be combined in different equations to give access to some very complicated behaviours. Good target training and planning opens up a whole new range of easily taught behaviours.

Targets are mostly employed as temporary teaching tools, but can be replaced with new cues at any time. As temporary teaching aids their use facilitates understanding and acquisition of the final cue which is stronger because the target will disappear.

As temporary teaching aids, targets need to be taught with the same motivation as for the final behaviour. If teaching a sendaway, or go to station, then the speed of the behaviour may be a critical part of the final behaviour. A mat is ideal for this and during learning, speed to the mat, with directness and commitment must be achieved if that is the action to be transferred to the final cue.

Keep a good record of your targets. Make sure they are clearly visible and easily discriminated by the dog. The Border Collies can discriminate between two balls - a golf ball and a ping-pong ball. The Gordons can also discriminate, but by scent, rather than sight. Which means they need to be much closer to smell the target. Their vision is suited for long distance, they do not watch their prey for tiny movements as the collies do. In fact we have no test as yet for optical weakness, just use your common sense and assess the dog's ability to recognise different objects. Do not rely on different colours, variety in shape and material is safer.

TARGET STICKS

A target stick needs an object on the end. A stick without a specific "touch" zone will not develop precision teaching. Once an object has been taught to a specific body part, a paw, nose, chin, etc., the object can be transferred to the target stick allowing an extension to your arm. This is ideal for the very small and very large dogs, and teaching an action with a target stick reduces the body language. Our body movements can inhibit the action, with crowding, poor balance or pressure by proximity.

Select objects with their future use in mind. A ball on a target stick needs to be clearly visible and easily discriminated from other objects. A specific scent may help when used as a nose target. Different foods can be used as targets, as can different objects.

The object targets will usually be free shaped and then used in a variety of ways to stimulate different behaviours. Nose target can be attached to hands, drawers, doors, sticks, crates etc., indicating "this is where your nose will go". A creative range of attachments will be needed: clips, pegs, poster tacks, sticky tacks, etc.

FREE SHAPING OBJECT ASSOCIATION

Object association will be much stronger when free shaped than if lured or handled. The dog becomes self aware of their own small actions which is a skill that is highly desirable in target training. The target itself will become the cue for that body part, the nose, front left paw, hips etc, and have a strong response when presented.

REWARD FOR ACTIONS

When free shaping small movement, make sure the reward is delivered to maintain action. For instance teaching a paw contact, the dog will need to be balanced on their other three legs to be able to repeat the action fluently. The action incorporates a change of balance, it is an essential part of the successful movement. When the object is presented it should initially stimulate a change of balance to free up the movement of the correct paw. Make sure the reward is delivered so that the dog can initiate this balancing action.

If the dog is confident to make and maintain contact with the object, the main-tenance can be clicked and rewards delivered in this position. Movement to elicit this outcome can be backchained into the contact point.

If the dog is unable to make contact initially, gradually increasing movements need to be taught. This will begin with the balance shift, then a light paw, then a lift of the paw etc. Reinforcement must be delivered to encourage repetition of the action and build confidence and self awareness skills. More accuracy can be attained through teaching the process step by step rather than using the outcome. A young dog may get a click for a paw tap, but the next contact may be a paw whack, which sends the object flying, or a paw push or pull.

Use the clicker to mark the opening balance shift and inhibit progression until there is evidence of self control. Then very gradually let the dog move their paw closer to the contact point, at a rate you can mark the correct actions. If the action deviates then return to the balance shift action.

After the click, use the food reward to lure the dog back to the standing, or sitting position. This is the opening position that the behaviour initiates from. A toss of the food behind the dog will require the dog to re-locate itself before beginning the change of balance action. This is an advanced criteria.

Once the confidence or self control is obtained, contact with the object, as an outcome, can be rewarded.

When using an object to stimulate an outcome, the reward can be given in situ. For example teaching the dog to stand on a mat. The dog will be clicked for standing on the mat, and fed in that location, for 15-20 repetitions. As the criteria is increased the reward food will be used to lure the dog a very small distance away from the mat. This will elicit the action to move to the mat. The click occurs on the successful outcome, but the reward is now placed at the opening location.

THE REWARD CLOCK

To avoid confusion the directional throw or placement of the reward will be used as in a clock. It will be assumed that you are always at 6 o'clock, the dog in the centre of the clock.

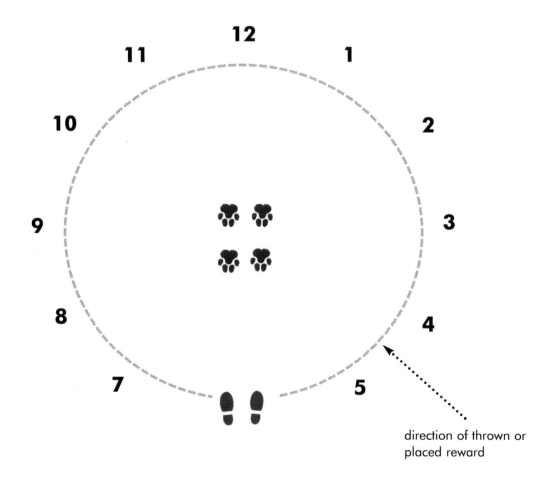

direction of thrown or placed reward

OBJECT	BODY PART	ACTION repertoire
Small Ball	Nose touch	Touch nose to, to push with nose, hold a pose, follow when moving, touch to indicate "this person", "this place". (page 31)
Flat small mat, such as mouse mat	Chin resting	To settle, for grooming or husbandry to the face. (page 43)
Jar lid, flat disc, beer mat, coaster	Different one for each paw	To place, to push, to tap, to pull, to wave, or for husbandry to the feet. (page 32)
Carpet sample mat	Front feet	To stand "four square" on, distance work, locations, stay still. (page 34)
Torch light	Eyes or scenting	Look in this direction, keep your body still. Achieve a head turn over a distance, look to indicate (drugs etc). (page 42)
Tug cloth, plaited	Mouth	Hold this, open drawer, pull, collect, retrieve, place. (page 38)
Cone, marker, pole	Flank, go around, cone to your side	Go to the left of, to the right of, go around in a circle, stand by the side of. (page 40)
Bedding	Whole body in down position	Lying down, sleep, settle, wait your turn.
Fencing, wall, barrier	Path of movement	Trot by the side, walk along, run around.
Plastic Piping, fly swat	Hips or back legs	Move into this sensation on your hips, teaching backing, moving left or right with hips.
Book, low brick or brick paver	Back feet	Step up onto, hold a position. (page 44)

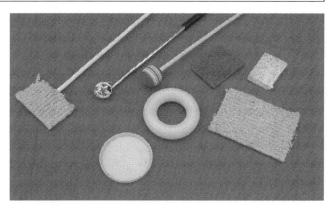

GAME 3:1 | Target: NEW LEARNER | LEVEL 1

Developing:
SELF AWARENESS
SELF CONTROL
MEMORY SKILLS

PREVIOUS SKILLS
None.

This exercise is an excellent first learning exercise for a young dog or dogs new to free shaping.

Select a suitable object that is highly likely to stimulate the desired attachment. Objects that are new elicit a sniff, (for nose attachment), on the floor elicit a paw tap or a flat mat for a chin.

New learners must be encouraged to offer all variety of interactions, experienced dogs can learn more specific actions sooner.

RESOURCES
Paw or Nose Object.

PATTERN OF PROGRESS Steps of increasing criteria   CLICK to mark   REWARD location

1.	Take a seat and open the lesson with several reinforcers for standing in front of you waiting for the lesson. Warm up the dog mentally, ensure concentration and focus.	Standing alert and focussed on you.	Thrown in random directions.

Throw the food to ensure the dog moves out of position to assess the dog's readiness, focus and desire to learn when they return to the "lesson is beginning" position

2.	Take the object, add plenty of your scent, talk to the object to encourage curiosity. Place the object directly in front of the dog.	Looking or focus on object.	Opening position.

Give the reward close to the object, but not at the contact point. Use the food to move the dog to the opening position.

3.	Showing interest, curiosity or desire to interact. Encourage interaction, in a new learner of any sort, then begin to exclude unwanted action by setting up the opening position to encourage the desired action only.	Correct action.	Opening position that encourages wanted behaviour.
4.	Build fluent, repetitive actions attaching the muscle collection to the presence of the object	Increasing fluency and confidence.	Opening position.
5.	Generalise the approach to the object. Begin to gradually change the location of the reward to extend flexible opening location. ie: turning to face the object, walking up to the object etc	Correct action	Variable locations for broadening the experience of arriving at the object

GAME 3:2 — Target: BALL NOSE — LEVEL 1

Developing:

REACTION ON TARGET CUE

SELF AWARENESS

This is a fundamental learning exercise that becomes the basis for teaching movement by following a target. Luring can seem to effect the same results, nose targets give a more secure demonstration of the learned behaviours.

The object needs the potential to be attached to a stick, carried in the hand, or at a place of nose contact - such as pushing a door.

PREVIOUS SKILLS

None.

RESOURCES

Nose target, with some scent for easy locating. Easily visible on most backgrounds.

PATTERN OF PROGRESS Steps of increasing criteria

Steps of increasing criteria	CLICK to mark	REWARD location
1. Place the ball target at nose height to the dog. Either temporarily on another object, or at the end of a stick.	Sniffing showing curiosity.	Near ball.
2. Build degree of contact with regular touch. The dog should be stationary when touching.	Contact with nose.	Near ball, but increasing the gap.
If the dog bites the ball, click to inhibit enthusiasm, and then look for a closed mouth approach.	Approach and then controlled approach.	Throw behind the dog.
3. Generalise with reward food thrown to random points around object, and object gradually changing height.	Contact with nose.	Random locations.

First learning the touch, which then leads to the "follow".

GAME 3:3

Target: DISC PAW

LEVEL 1

Developing:
  SMALL ACTIONS
  LEFT FROM RIGHT
  CONTROLLED BALANCE

PREVIOUS SKILLS
Target: New Learner 3:1

This is a fundamental learning exercise that becomes the basis for many variations and advanced behaviours.

4   learning to differentiate between left and right paw

4   learning to control type of action, ie:
       height (wave, tap)
       intensity (pull, push)
       which part of the paw (pad, nail, top)

RESOURCES
Two small, different low, shaping articles, such as jar lids, saucer.

PATTERN OF PROGRESS Steps of increasing criteria	CLICK to mark	REWARD location
1. Shape the dog to hold a position by the object, with focus on the object.	Opening position, suitable for action.	Opening position.
2. Select the action of the favoured paw, and ignore actions with the other foot.	Click only the chosen paw.	Floor, behind the chosen paw.

placement of the food can make it easier for the paw to be free to move. Consider the balance point needed for either paw

3. Shape the action, a light tap, a push, or a pull.	Correct action.	Reset to comfortable standing position
4. To increase height, raise the object on a book or brick. Ensure that the object faces the part of the paw to make contact. If you are shaping a paw wave the object must become vertical when raised to the dog's eye level.	The action when contact is made.	Reset to comfortable standing position.

Note: this target must be unique for this paw. Its location will dictate the type of action.

5. Change targets and teach a repeat process with the other front paw.	Click correct paw & action.	Reset to encourage selected paw.

ADVANCED BEHAVIOURS FROM TARGET: FRONT PAWS

Both feet at the same time. Place both targets in the location to trigger the desired action:
>   side by side for a double paw push
>   at dog's eye level for both high paws

Transfer the target to the new object:
>   hold the target in the palm of your hand
>   place the target on your shoe
>   place the target on a press button
>   place the target over the scent for indication

Teaching a cross over of one leg over the other when lying down. Place the target for the left paw on the other side of the right paw.

Teaching a different range of actions.

Use a different object for each action, initially pairing the object used to teach each paw with the action object. ie: lid + brick = wave, brick then becomes "left paw wave".

Other actions:
>   PUSH - using flat object on smooth surface, encourage touch with a standing balance
>   PULL - place the object further away, encourage the balance point backwards, or lock into the sit position
>   FLICK - use a cup, or beaker, place very close to the dog's paw, cue the lift, click when beaker falls over. Contact point would be the top of the paw
>   HOLD WITH BOTH FEET - in the down position, attach a cord to a precious toy, and pull upwards when under both paws

ADD THE VERBAL CUE

Although the two targets for left and right can be perpetually used to transfer the matching foot to different actions, the use of verbal cues will prove very useful when teaching the dog to differentiate between Left actions and Right actions. The dog can learn to Spin Left, Step Right, Jump Left, Retrieve Right in the future.

| GAME 3:4 | **Target: MAT FEET** | LEVEL 2 |

Developing:
STANDING TOUCH
CHANGING SENSATION
LOCATION AWARENESS

PREVIOUS SKILLS
Target: New Learner 3:1

This is an excellent exercise for teaching contact with an object, where the object is the outcome.

Many different behaviours can be taught by setting different situations and cues transitioned from the mat.

The mat must be a different sensation to the surrounding floor. Initially the dog may learn the mat behaviour through the changing sensation of the different surface under their feet, before recognising the mat.

RESOURCES
Carpet samples, flat plates, rubber mats etc.

PATTERN OF PROGRESS Steps of increasing criteria | **CLICK** to mark | **REWARD** location

Place the mat directly in front of your chair, at least an arm's length away. You should be able to just feed the dog when standing on the mat without leaving your chair.

PATTERN OF PROGRESS	CLICK to mark	REWARD location
1. Click as the dog arrives on the mat, toss the food almost simultaneously. This will discourage the dog from walking through the mat, on click the food goes behind them.	Arriving on mat.	Behind the dog, at 12 o'clock. (see page 28)
2. As the dog arrives on the mat, withhold the click for 2 seconds to ensure the dog is standing still.	On mat and standing still.	Behind the dog, at 12 o'clock.
3. Changing the location of the reward to 10/11o'clock, or 1/2 o'clock. Look for the dog returning towards you a positive deviation to the mat. Ensure the dog has learned "going onto the mat" and not "walking towards you".	On mat and standing still.	Behind the dog, to assess learned behaviour.
4. Move the mat slightly closer for several repetitions and slightly further away to ensure a good generalisation of "arriving on the mat and standing still".	On mat and standing still.	Behind or to the side of the dog, to assess learned behaviour.
5. Change the location of the mat and the reward, where the reward is in front of you and the dog turns away to go to the mat. Two behaviours will be taught - looking for the mat, and going to the mat.	On mat and standing still.	In front of you, or tossed behind you for additional acceleration.

ADVANCED BEHAVIOURS FROM TARGET MAT FEET

HOLD YOUR POSITION

Cue the dog to go to the mat, and instead of throwing the reward away, move towards the dog to feed in location. A different click can be used to indicate a lack of activity, as opposed to the standard click which signals a movement to get the food reward.

The dog can be cued to a different position, and the mat indicate a "hold your place and position", until the behaviour is on cue.

WORK AT A DISTANCE

Cue the dog to go to the mat, and throw the food some distance away. The dog should be able to travel towards the mat with you in proximity to the mat (A) before you begin to step away from the mat(B). Very slowly build the distance, click when the dog arrives, and encourage speed and commitment with the thrown / chase rewards.

Once running to the mat, cue the "hold your position cue", and give the cue for another behaviour. Click and reward on the mat.

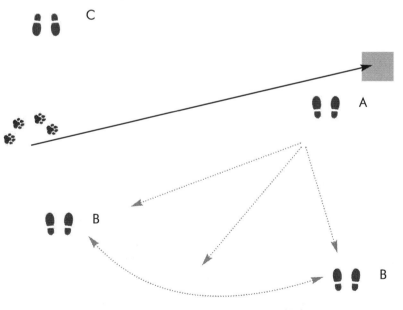

ADD THE CUE

The mat itself is its own cue, which continually speaks to the dog "come here" or "stand on me". A verbal cue can be added to indicate that the dog should travel towards the mat, ie. leave you. Additional cues can be given once the dog has arrived.

GAME 3:5 — Target: STICK — LEVEL 2

Developing:
SMALL ACTIONS
LEFT FROM RIGHT
CONTROLLED BALANCE

PREVIOUS SKILLS
Target stationary objects
3:2, 3:3, 3:4.

Placing a target object on the end of a stick allows us to separate the behaviour from our own body movements. This results in making the transition to the final cue easier

Most objects can be used on a stick: the ball nose, the disc paw, or used in conjunction with mat feet, carry this way, place here, push this etc.

The key to success is to ensure the dog is fully focussed on the object, not you or the stick. Keep your body language to a minimum.

RESOURCES
Telescopic lightweight stick, attachable objects.

PATTERN OF PROGRESS Steps of increasing criteria	CLICK to mark	REWARD location

	CLICK to mark	REWARD location
1. Refresh the object with the correct interaction, and then ask for several repetitions when attached to the stick.	Correct interaction.	Near object.

At this point the object is a cue. Make sure the object and the stick are out of sight as soon as the click occurs. If the object is constantly present there is too much possibility that the dog will not respond on first presentation of the cue object. This would be the same as continually cueing sit sit sit sit sit, until the dog responded.
Good cue response is prompt and without hesitation. The dog should respond as soon as the object is brought into view.

HIGH FIVES - DISC PAW

1. Choosing a stationary position, sit or down, use the paw (left or right) object on the stick, begin with a low level touch contact and gradually build height.	Paw contact.	In opening position.
2. Shape until the dog is at full extension with one paw, but not jumping. Put on cue and then match with synchronised hand contact.	Paw contact and no jump.	In opening position.

BUMP OR PUSH - BALL NOSE

Once good contact is established with ball using a target stick very gradually move the ball away. The dog will need to respond with several touches or push into the ball to maintain the contact.	More intense push against ball.	Near ball.

ADVANCED BEHAVIOURS FROM TARGET

FOLLOW

1. As the dog approaches the ball begin to move the target away, click for movement towards the target as it moves	Following the target.	Thrown away to encourage movement

Do not try to teach moving contact, this is far too hard. When following, the dog should be focussed on the target, but not touching. Movement can be completed with a stationary target that the dog can finally contact.

2. Keep the speed of the moving target within the dog's level of competence. Gradually increase speed when fluency is demonstrated.	Following the target AND focus on target.	Thrown far away to encourage faster movement to target.
3. Generalise with changing height and speeds.	Following the target AND focus on target.	Thrown away.

When teaching the dog to following a target you are building a trust that this behaviour will not result in tripping, bumping into other objects or unsafe proximity to another dog.

From the FOLLOW exercise you can teach:
  different gaits (see 4:12, page 80)
  different movement patterns
  movements around you, leg weaving etc.
  go over jumps, weaving poles, search items etc.
  small dogs can learn their heel position
  go over the jump or obstacle

LIMPING

The paw target can be used to teach the dog to walk with one foot in the air, either as a "poorly paw" (low held up), or as a "high paw". Take the transition from stationary touch to moving touch with care, as the balance will present a challenge for the dog.

TRANSFER TO NEW OBJECTS: CHANGE THE CUE

The target disc paw, or ball nose, can be used to teach the dog to touch new objects, such as pushing a button, shutting a drawer, focussing on a judge. Refresh the target behaviour, and then make contact with the new target. Add the new cue and transition the behaviour when the dog anticipates your movement of the target.

GAME 3:6

Target: CLOTH HOLD

LEVEL 2

Developing:
RETRIEVE
CARRY AND ASSISTANCE

PREVIOUS SKILLS
Follow with hand or object (4:12 page 80).
Combining targets (3:12 page 48).

Nearly all target training is a foundation behaviour for a limitless range of more advanced or complex behaviours.

Depending on the dog's enthusiasm and experience a mouth grab is fairly easy to elicit. This is a natural behaviour to young puppies of all breeds. The more the prey instincts are aroused the more likely the dog is to grab the cloth target.

RESOURCES
Cloth target, suitable to contain food and retrieve objects.

PATTERN OF PROGRESS Steps of increasing criteria

PATTERN OF PROGRESS Steps of increasing criteria	CLICK to mark	REWARD location
1. Using the method on page 130 to teach the tug, begin to replace a good grab on the sock with the food from your hand supply. Repeat until dogs responds immediately to sight of sock.	Click for grabbing the sock.	Off the item. From hand supply of food.
2. Begin to fill the sock with items of other size, weight and texture (one at a time!), knot behind the new item. The sock will grow in size with the tugging, or you can transfer to a fabric bag.	For grabbing sock and new item.	Off the item. From hand supply of food.
3. Once the dog has generalised the fabric, transition onto new objects by attaching the fabric to other items. Sew a section around the grip bar of a dumbbell, telephone, etc.	Taking hold of new object over indicated area.	Off the item. From hand supply of food.
4. To teach the dog to carry the object extend the duration of a stationary hold beyond the time taken for travelling. Then using a target stick nose follow, cue the dog to carry and follow.	Movement with the object.	At the opening position by the retrieve object.
5. To teach the dog to take an object to a place or location, use the target mat, cue carry and follow to mat.	Moving the object to the mat.	At the opening position by the retrieve object.

ADVANCED BEHAVIOURS FROM TARGET: CLOTH HOLD

NEW OBJECTS

The dog can be taught to carry new objects with the transition cloth, or the new objects placed on the transition cloth.

PULL TO OPEN

A tug object can be attached to a cupboard or drawer and the dog cued to pull the object to open the drawer, or remove clothing.

Use a different object for pull if carry is also going to be taught.

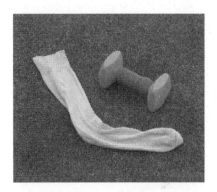

ADD THE CUE

Cues can be added to indicate "carry this object". The cloth itself is the "old cue". Each object can be named as required for discrimination, such as the toys, or household items: telephone, walking stick, glasses etc. The location, where the dog should carry the object to, can be added. This is taught with the target mat.

GAME 3:7 | Target: CONE POLE | LEVEL 2

Developing:

SELF AWARE MOVEMENT

FOLLOWING A PATTERN

DISCRIMINATING LEFT FROM RIGHT

PREVIOUS SKILLS

Experience of various targeting behaviours: nose, paw etc.

This object will trigger a particular movement: "pass the side of your body around this object".

A foundation behaviour for teaching a dog to move in a large circle, go around an object and hold a position, circle an object, use an object as a distance marker.

Use a different object to indicate "pass on your left", or "pass on your right" to the dog.

Circling an object can also be taught with a target stick and nose follow, but learning to interact with an object as movement, rather than a contact is an important learning strategy of self awareness.

RESOURCES

Different cones, or fixed poles.

PATTERN OF PROGRESS Steps of increasing criteria	CLICK to mark	REWARD location
1. Place the object on the floor, at arm's length in front of you, with a reward tossed off to 12 o'clock (1# diagram 1 opposite). Use the probability of the dog moving towards you as an opportunity to click as they pass by the cone.	Flank passing by the object. (Of the dog's choosing, but consistent).	Tossed away, increasing the degree of curve (diagram 1)
2. Gradually increase the section of the circle that the dog completes by careful placement of the reward. The hardest part is when the dog curves between you and the cone and turns their head away to go around the back.	Increasing duration of the movement with the flank nearest the cone.	To increase duration.
3. Using several repetitions of the 5th pattern, then keep the shape, but move the reward location back towards the 12 o'clock position, maintaining the behaviour pattern.	Increase curve, and turning away from you.	Setting same behaviour but new location.

If the dog finds the pattern difficult to acquire, use a target mat placed by the cone, and the same reward location pattern to encourage the circle action.

DIAGRAM 1

= order of
reward treat

dog's path of return

1#
2#
3#
4#
5#

click when in
this area

you are
sitting here

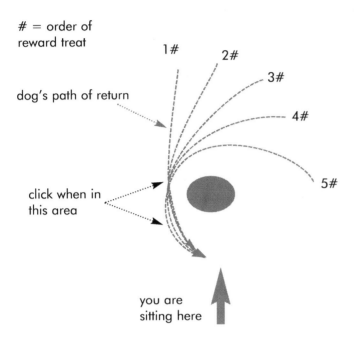

DIAGRAM 2

13#
14#
15#
6-12#

click when in this
area (or place a
mat here)

you are
sitting here

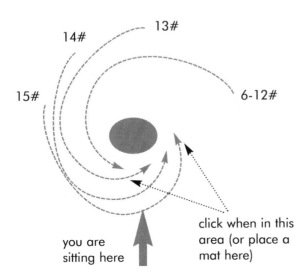

GAME 3:8

Target: EYES

Developing:
SELF CONTROL
MICRO MOVEMENT
SELF AWARENESS

This target will teach the dog to look at a particular target, and sustain the behaviour.

The easiest way to stimulate this is to place an object on the end of a target that will move with the slightest wiggle of the target stick, or alternately use a light to flash on and off.

PREVIOUS SKILLS
Maintain your station (stay).

RESOURCES
Target light, or target feather on end of stick.

PATTERN OF PROGRESS Steps of increasing criteria	CLICK to mark	REWARD location
1. Begin with the dog "on station" such as sitting on a small stool, box or mat. Flick the item, or light on, and wiggle around until the dog looks at the object.	For looking.	Maintaining station.
2. Use fairly large movements to encourage the dog to maintain their focus.	For sustaining the look.	Maintaining station.
3. Gradually reduce the movement until the look, or mark, is maintained.	For sustaining the look, or mark.	Maintaining station.

The behaviour can be transferred to new objects, and put on cue. Useful for photography, marking a person or thrown object.

GAME 3:9

Target: CHIN

Developing:
ACTION OF HEAD
RELAXED POSTURE

This is a useful exercise when taught with a mat or palm of hand.

The objects need to be only as large as the dog's chin area, a cut down mouse mat is quite suitable.

PREVIOUS SKILLS
Down Sleepy (6:2 page 111)

RESOURCES
A Chin mat.

PATTERN OF PROGRESS Steps of increasing criteria	CLICK to mark	REWARD location
1. From the Sleepy Down place a mat where the dog will drop its head to the floor.	Contact with the mat.	Lying down, but the head upright.
2. Once confident, transfer to a standing position and the mat placed on a chair or in the palm of your hand.	Contact with the mat.	Lying down, but the head upright.

This exercise is a good foundation for husbandry, or teaching a dog to have its face examined in the show ring.

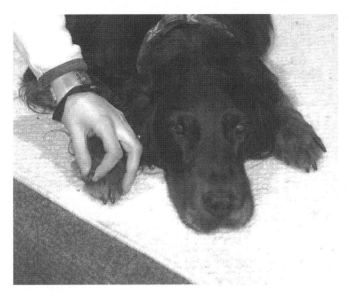

GAME 3:10 | Target: BOOK | LEVEL 2

Developing:
SMALL ACTIONS
HIGH DEGREE OF SELF AWARENESS
VERY CONTROLLED BALANCE

This exercise requires a high degree of self awareness, and develops good memory skills.

4   learning to focus on an insensitive part of body

4   learning to maintain difficult balance and control subtle movement

This is a difficult exercise for some dogs. Movement of the back legs and paw takes a high degree of self awareness.

PREVIOUS SKILLS
Good standing balance awareness of non-visual target.

RESOURCES
Small low brick or paver, low staircase or book.

PATTERN OF PROGRESS Steps of increasing criteria	CLICK to mark	REWARD location
1. Begin with a standing position and place the target object close behind, or to the side of, one of the dog's rear legs.	Any initial contact.	Reset opening standing position.

Initially shape a fidgeting standing position and note which direction the dog's back legs are inclined to move. This maybe backwards or sideways. Place the back paw target object in the path of the likely movement.

2. Increase regular contact with the target until solid contact.	Specific type of contact.	Reset opening standing position.
3. Reset the target to control the desired movement.	Solid contact.	Reset opening standing position.

VARIATIONS

Both feet at the same time. Place both targets in the location to trigger the desired action.

Virginia Broitman very successfully demonstrated with her Miniature Pinscher that a dog can be taught back leg targets, and when placed up a wall taught to do a hand stand (standing on front legs) with the rear legs up the wall. Cool one!

To teach one leg to lift, as if cocking a leg to urinate, place the target higher, and out to the side of the dog.

Make sure the dog is encourage to bring their balance forward, with a lowering of the head.

A neck scratch can be taught through a rear leg target.

Attach the target to a target stick, and with the dog in a settled down position, bring the target foot closer to the next with the target stick placement.

Once achieved in the down, transfer to the sit and standing positions.

ADD THE VERBAL CUE

A verbal cue is critical for this behaviour, and will prevent the dog turning around to look for the targets.

GAME 3:11

Target: GO FROM A TO B

LEVEL 1

Developing:
CONTROLLED FOCUS
MOVEMENT TO TARGET
CHANGING TARGETS

This Game teaches a dog to move between targets. The targets can be either two mats, or objects, or two people.

Once the dog is moving with confidence and fluently, behaviours can be inserted "enroute" between the targets, such as a jump, or obstacle or cavaletti, or for practising recalls between two people.

PREVIOUS SKILLS
Mat Feet (3:4 page 34).

RESOURCES
Two mats or two teachers, person A and person B.

PATTERN OF PROGRESS Steps of increasing criteria

PATTERN OF PROGRESS Steps of increasing criteria	CLICK to mark	REWARD location
1. Two teachers, each with a supply of food rewards and a clicker, stand approximately 2m (6 foot) apart. Build up a to and fro behaviour, but avoid prompting the dog to move between each person.	Engaging with person, looking at their face, hands or food.	Thrown to the feet of other person. A throws to feet of person B, B to person A etc.
2. Change the reward location to in front of the person that has just clicked the dog for engaging with them. Now the dog must initiate the disengagement with that person (A), and move towards the person that has clicked (B).	Disengagement from one person (A) and look at the other person (B).	On arrival at second person (B)
3. Build the fluency moving from one person to another. The dog should begin to anticipate changing people, and possibly eating as they progress to the other person. Appropriate to the dog's level of confidence, begin to move the two teachers apart.	Looking at other person.	On arrival at other person.
4. The click can be changed to meet new criteria such as the dog beginning to move at speed, or over further distances.	The dog initiating a change in behaviour.	On arrival at other person.

VARIATIONS

SINGLE TEACHER, TWO MATS

The same process can be taught between two target mats, with a single teacher. As the food is placed on the target mat the dog is at (A), the teacher begins to move to the other target mat (B), and waits for the dog to arrive. With this variation the dog is rewarded for arriving, not engaging.

The cue to move to the other mat is the teacher's body language. The dog will begin to anticipate that the target mat to move to is the one the teacher is facing.

The behaviour can be put on a self running cue, ie, as soon as the dog has reached one target mat, they automatically move themselves to the other target mat. (If you intend to teach the dog to maintain a position on a target then use unique targets to teach this automatic change-target behaviour.) A verbal cue can also be used.

Both strategies would allow the teacher to stand at any place relative to the dog whilst the dog moves over obstacles etc. independent of the teacher's body language.

RUN ALONGSIDE HANDLER - 2 NEW TEACHERS

If the handler wishes to be able to move at speed by the side of the dog, it is recommendable to use new teachers for running from A to B, not one of the teacher's later becoming the handler.

RECALL AROUND THE RING

This enables a dog to practise a recall on name, a group of people can place themselves in a ring approximately 4m, or 12 feet, apart. After the dog has learned to move between two people on their name and a "here" cue, more people can be added.

SHOW TO A JUDGE

This same technique can be used to teach a dog to gait towards a person when on lead beside the handler. This gives the dog a target person to focus on, which is ideal for the show ring.

ADD THE CUE

The dog's name can precede the disengagement, once the behaviour is fluent.

GAME 3:12 — Target: COMBINATIONS — LEVEL 3

Developing:
COMPLEX BEHAVIOURS
LATERAL THINKING

Targets are our language with the dog. If each target is carefully acquired and understood we can begin to combine targets and actions into sentences.

Normally the syntax will be:

> your body part 4 action 4 location

SUGGESTED COMBINATIONS

1. Carry this article and place it on this location:

tidy the toys away
place in basket, carry basket to here

2. Pull this target

open the draw
fetch the article placed in the drawer
ring bell to alert or request door opening

3. Push your nose against the target:

shut the door, drawer, cupboard

4. Back up with this item with your mouth:

switch on the light, pull off my sock

5. Follow the mats along the floor in this pattern:

move in a circle,
over obstacles

6. Search the area around the end of the target stick:

search and indicate on substance.

7. Take this article to a specific person:

deliver the post

8. Go place a paw on a specific person:

go find Daddy, tea is ready

9. "Let me introduce you to:"

look at this person, offer a raised paw

10. Heelwork:

trot in this style in this position next to me

11. Go to sit on the box, wave your left paw

"box, sit, paw left"

4 GAMES
Movement

We are all aware that exercise is an important part of a healthy lifestyle and promotes longevity. There have been times when taking the dog out for a good walk was the solution to reduce the dog's energy level and allow us to maintain our own busy lifestyle. This only works short term as the fitter the dog becomes the more exercise it takes to settle them.

An average dog needs daily exercise. In fact, people are probably more aware of their dog's need for a daily walk than their own. Most dogs are designed for regular and challenging activity to maintain them in good health. For sports, or

working dogs, it is our responsibility to ensure we develop dogs with more than just the skills for the job, but a fitness level and well developed and supporting muscle structures that enhance the activity, prevent injury and early retirement.

I began teaching my dogs Heelwork to Music and Freestyle in 1996. The dogs came from a background of competitive obedience, hill sheepdogs, search dogs and ordinary pet dogs. Over the years we developed a repertoire of freestyle moves such as spins, turns, weaving, backing, beg, side stepping, collected trots, paw work etc. Heelwork was duplicated on the right side as well as the left.

It became apparent, that despite having "fit" dogs, ie. dogs that were field fit, that could run after balls, birds or sheep, take long, country walks and work in hot weather; they were not well developed with flexibility or balanced movement. The heelwork dogs were uncomfortable on the opposite side. So was I!

Over the years I have developed a range of exercises that maintain fluid, balanced movements, are always jerk free and without stress, build strength gradually and with a result that now my elderly dogs are fit and mobile well into their old age. The competition dogs are able to maintain high energy and stamina for much longer, continue active competition to an older age and the Gordon Setters are especially mobile for a large breed.

None of these movements are unnatural. They exist as part of the normal development of puppies, often in preparation for the opportunity for sex. When dogs are flirting they perform some extreme movements to elicit interest or demonstrate their fine provider potential (think disco dance floors).

TYPE OF FITNESS AND EXERCISE

There are two types of exercise: AEROBIC and ANAEROBIC.

AEROBIC exercise develops and maintains cardiovascular fitness: strengthening the heart, improving the capacity of the lungs and controling weight. Canine aerobic exercise is dog jogging (trotting, or slow canter at an easy pace), field running (hunting), field cruising (mooching around at variable speeds), swimming, playing ball or fetching.

The dog's level of fitness will depend on the breed, the terrain, the heat and lifestyle. Most dogs can benefit from 3/4 sessions a week, or 10 - 20 minutes aerobic exercise. They should not be pushed to exhaustion or exercised in hot conditions.

During aerobic exercise a dog's active muscles perform hundreds of repetitions with a relatively low load or resistance. This is ineffective for developing flexibility or specific muscle tone. The terrain can influence the level of resistance, such as running around sand dunes, heavy mud or hilly ground where repetitively used muscles, such as thigh muscles, will become larger and harder.

ANAEROBIC exercise focuses on specific muscles and their size, endurance, and strength. Weight lifting and resistance training are examples of human anaerobic exercise. This area would be suitable for career sports and working dogs, where specialised plans should be drawn up to build the required muscles.

STRETCHING can significantly improve flexibility in a given period of time. It is ideal for everyday movements to maintain the flexibility that young dogs possess throughout their lives.

FLEXIBILITY is defined as the range of possible movement in a joint and its surrounding muscles; stretching and flexibility exercises can help restore the motion of the joint to its normal range.

Muscular fitness is a combination of strength, endurance and flexibility.

EXERCISE PROGRAMMES

A balanced programme will include a warm up to begin, the relevant exercises to maintain flexibility or develop specific strengths and a cool down on completion. This will be complemented with 3 or 4 regular aerobic walks a week on variable surfaces.

1. WARM UP / COOL DOWN

Begin with a general warm-up of 3-4 minutes gentle trot. Warming up gradually increases the heart rate and blood flow and raises the temperature of muscles, ligaments and tendons. Stretching while muscles are cold may injure muscles. When cooling down take the dog through a slower version of the warm up with some Everyday Exercises.

2. EVERYDAY EXERCISES

Follow with a range of Everyday Exercises to maximise the circulation to the general muscle groups.

3. SPORTS EXERCISE

Move onto mimicking the Sports Exercises, such as a slow circle for freestyle, or a low jump for agility, and then move the dog into stretching the muscles by opposing the action. For circles and spins, hold the dog in the spin or circle position, in both directions, extend the elbow with support for jumping, hold each position for 5 - 15 seconds.

4. Then work on the selected Sports Exercises that develop strength and endurance followed by the cool down.

FLEXIGILITY

This is a programme I designed to develop the young dog, socially challenged dogs and dogs recovering from injury or physically under developed. Gordon Setters have a reputation for a low level of body awareness. They bump into furniture, collide regularly on walks, sometimes with me, and can even miss when jumping up to greet. It is part of their appeal, but special attention to developing body awareness through Flexi-gility training improves this enormously.

A series of low level planks and other pieces of equipment are used to teach a dog to walk under control, sit, down, turn around, step backwards. For a 9 months old, male gordon Setter, this is a major challenge. The plank is only the width of his stride, and on level ground he is clear to sit as he wants, lie down as he wants and turn around in as large a space as possible. By transferring these skills to the constraints of a plank the dog has to exert more control over the fine muscles that perform these everyday skills.

This has proved very beneficial to learning all types of movements. The dogs become more aware of their bodies and are able to use them with greater control. Many of our class dogs that find it difficult to communicate with other dogs and are likely to fear the proximity of strange dogs, also find Flexi-gility exercises hard to perform. It is one area of exercise that these often tense dogs learn to enjoy, and begin to share the enjoyable experience with other dogs.

Flexi-gility also gives dogs different physical experiences. A range of surfaces, that wobble, slip, odd angles, new sensations, that demand co-ordination and balance and build flexibility for future, unknown experiences. They develop skills of adaptation.

COMMON SENSE

All movement exercises will need you to use your very best common sense. Where possible stay in physical contact with the dog so you can feel the tension and levels of comfort or discomfort building up. Watch the dog's face for a flicker of pain, or a resistance to move. If you are physically manipulating, luring or motivating a dog beyond its choice you MUST be diligent in building slowly and sensibly. Some dogs are ruled by their stomach or play desire and will ignore their own pain. Giving free choice in movement allows the dog to display discomfort or the degree of effort it takes, and the choice to stop after a number of repetitions.

Avoid too vigorous stretching, stretching until it hurts, or holding the stretch too long. Stretching should feel good. The dog should be relaxed and confident. Ideally capture that stretch the dog performs when waking up - the walk forward play bow, arching the back, the roll of the head and neck, stretching each back leg out behind, a little shake, a tail up and over ... and be ready for the bowels to also have their little stretch as well. Phee-uw!

TEACHING EXERCISE AND MOVEMENTS

For either dog or person it is far easier to learn a movement than an absence of movement. 95% of what we teach with the clicker is an action and actions controlled by muscles.

This may vary from:

◆   a group of muscles, such as a drop to the floor from standing, involving compression of all leg joints and perhaps a dip of the head

◆   a simple muscle movement, such as a head turn, or tail wag

◆   a repetition of movement to develop flexibility or familiarity

◆   a sustained movement, such as pressing a paw against a target, or high stepping trotting action, equivalent to our weight lifting and developing strength

◆   a relaxation of muscle tension

Our skill lies in our ability to capture those specific collections, and successfully communicate this to the dog.

Our skill lies in our ability to capture those specific collections, and successfully communicate this to the dog.

Movements can be skillfully used to enhance a dog's quality of life and the free choice element that clicker training brings ensures we only ask the dog to offer these behaviours within its own sense of comfort and security.

MOVEMENTS ARE FLUID IN THEIR HISTORY

Movements have difficulty staying the same. Initially the movement will be controlled, exploratory and steady until the learner is clear what the action is. When familiarity arrives the movement will noticeably improve in fluency. With fluency a strength begins to build and the muscles develop their stretch and contraction capacity. With sustained duration the collectionof the muscles will begin to get stronger and develop a more pronounced movement. With opposition more strength will develop and supporting muscles will increase.

As we practice movements, it is their nature to change. Depending on what phase we want to maintain the movement we have to schedule our training to focus on that area.

For example. I strive for a trotting heel position. The dog is close and stepping out with a rhythmic, slightly exaggerated movement. The head is raised and the drive is from the rear legs. This takes many months of repetitive physical movement to build the muscles necessary to maintain this position for more than a handful of steps. I devise a whole series of exercises that build the muscles BEFORE there is any association with the heel position. I do not use the heel position to teach the muscle strength. During development there will naturally be some confusion, a possibility of discomfort or high excitement in the Sports Games. I may not want these emotions connected to the heel location. When the movement is free and unstressed, I combine it with the technical knowledge, taught without speed, of where the heel position is, and how to get to it: moving sideways, slightly forwards, slightly backwards, on the curve and through a pivot.

At the other extreme I use turning a small circle on the spot as a movement in freestyle and to maintain flexibility of the spine. I never want this movement to develop beyond a certain point. As the momentum of the movement increases the spin will lose control. Either the dog will move off position or rotate around

MOVEMENT IS NEVER STATIC

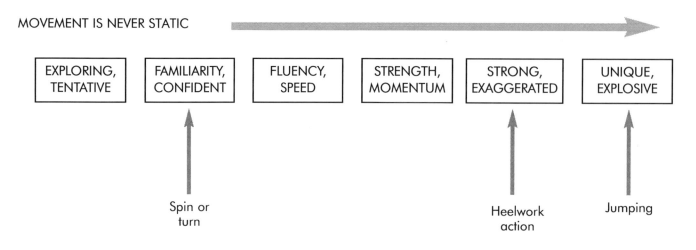

| EXPLORING, TENTATIVE | FAMILIARITY, CONFIDENT | FLUENCY, SPEED | STRENGTH, MOMENTUM | STRONG, EXAGGERATED | UNIQUE, EXPLOSIVE |

Spin or turn

Heelwork action

Jumping

the shoulders at a central point. With Border Collies there is an inclination to spin out of control when frustrated. In practice the movement is kept on the target stick, or with enclosing barriers to maintain the shape, and lack of speed.

TEACH COLLECTIONS OF MOVEMENTS

Building an athletic dog is a craft that skillfully employed will prevent injury and premature aging. Many dogs with high levels of activity will need to be protected from their own mental state. They may want to carry on playing ball and disregard pulled muscles telling them they should stop.

We can learn much from our own sports and professions about building athletes and dancers at the right age, with the appropriate movements and regular schedules to maintain the fundamental control and strength.

When teaching a dog movement, carefully plan the development and try to teach the movement as a slow version of the finished product, not teach isolated movements that come together when achieved.

Dancers will learn a slow synchronised movement of both their legs and arms at the same time, they will not learn just the feet or just the hands. The brain and nervous system will "collect" the instructions for the whole movement and store them during the acquisition phase with more efficiency than if individually acquired and merged at a later time. It is the nature of learning when under stress to revert to first acquisition.

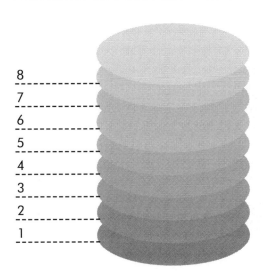

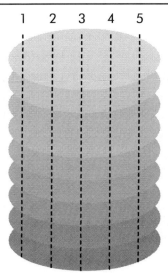

Clicker training teaching up through the layers, acquisition one behaviour at a time

Movement training working across all the layers, from slow acquisition of composite behaviours

This is somewhat in opposition to the standard clicker training strategy where small behaviours are broken down into tiny components to be taught. But where the muscle sets need to happen simultaneously plan to collect them together at the teaching phase.

EXERCISE PROGRAMMES

DEFINITIONS AND ASSESSMENT OF AGE GROUP

It is impossible to measure the exercise group a dog is suitable for by age alone. The larger breeds develop slowly and age chronologically sooner than the small breeds.

NURSERY GROUP: Pups that are able to physically run freely, roll around, play with siblings, tug, feed from a standing dam. In this group pups will gain significant, measurable growth weekly. For Border Collies this period ends at about 7 months, for Setters at 10 months.

Puppies will not have the required muscle strength for sustained activity of any one sort. Exercise needs to be balanced and of a gently gymnastic nature that comes from play.

Teaching a puppy a sit is an obvious necessity as a management tool, but because of the inclination of immature joints and muscles the action often results in a sloppy posture. This is one that we do not want to extend into adulthood. Everyday Sit exercises can begin to develop the correct muscles that mature into tight sits that are prompt and sustainable.

JUNIOR GROUP: Pups able to control movement, trot for short distances, hold a balanced sit (not floppy). Growth in height is minimal with growth finishing within the bones and some broadening of the chest and skull etc. For Border Collies this period ends at about 14 months, for Setters at 18 months.

This age group is in danger of looking like adults, wanting to have the activity of adults but only having a "soft", unfinished adult body. They should never have to tolerate the stresses an adult body is prepared for. No excessive aerobic or anaerobic exercise.

ADULT GROUP: Developing into full fitness, enjoying regular activities. Still looking for more action after 30 minutes free running. For Border Collies this period ends at about 10 years, for Setters at 9 years.

OLDER GROUP OR RECUPERATING DOGS: The dogs begin to slow down, on previously energetic walks they now walk alongside rather than free run before the end of the walk. Can experience some stiffness on getting up after exercise, may have reduced jumping desire. For Border Collies this period ends at about 13 years, for Setters at 11 years.

As with the Junior group this age group will have more intention than is healthy and need to be protected from a desire to overdo things.

ELDERLY GROUP: Still willing, but the body is definitely slowing down. Long walks are no longer a pleasure. Many hours spent sleeping. Maybe loosing sight and hearing, but with a willing appetite exercises can be induced. Always train on a soft surface, that provide good balance and grip, such as deep carpet or bedding. Make sure nail length is correct. Food maybe grabbed from the hand with poor eyesight, so use a "give the pony a nut" palm offer.

Young puppies are amazingly flexible. They seem to have rubber spines and enormous bounce in their leg joints. Play is designed as a mechanism for the brain to develop memories of specific behaviours. Some of these behaviours may never be called on but a young dog will practice them in play. They will fine tune their fighting skills, stalking prey, flesh ripping, neck breakers, critter chasing and motivating peers by teasing, indifference and "chill" skills. As they get older some of these actions will develop in specific movements and other actions will be lost.

If a dog is not regularly trotted the action can disappear. Perhaps when you lead walk your large dog it "walks" by your side without breaking into a trot. When free running the dog may spend most of the time cantering around or tracking birds. The stepping out trot can be lost. This is an essential skill that all dogs should use regularly to keep healthy and fit.

Designing a plan for a balanced collection of movements can keep the elderly dog free and mobile. These are not exaggerated movements, but a collection of everyday actions that can be lost through lifestyle neglect.

	NURSERY PROGRAMME	JUNIOR PROGRAMME	SENIOR / SPORT PROGRAMME	OLDER PROGRAMME	ELDERLY PROGRAMME
AEROBIC	none	gently building, never to exhaustion	as desirable for general fitness or work/sports	as comfortable	none
ANAEROBIC	natural sibling play in varied environments	natural play, with controlled equality	with specific work / sports plans	none	none
STRETCHING	none	none	yes	yes, as comfortable	yes, as comfortable
FLEXI-GILITY	learning balance and experiencing new surfaces	co-ordination in everyday movements	co-ordination in everyday movements	not necessary	none
EVERYDAY MOVEMENTS	only naturally offered movements	junior movements	work / sports dog movements	junior movements	those which are comfortable

| GAME 4:1 | **STRETCHES** | LEVEL 1 |

Developing:
MUSCLE TONE
CONFIDENT HANDLING
RELAXATION

Stretching is an important part of muscle development. Injury can be prevented from inappropriate or sudden extension to the muscles.

Some dogs will find some actions uncomfortable, so take great care to develop slowly and always build the dog's confidence that your hands will not cause them discomfort.

Beginning with very bendy young puppies is an ideal way to learn the canine body, and get the pup used to handling.

Three or four movements of each action is sufficient, holding for 3-5 seconds each time where comfortable.

1. Turning the head into the shoulder so stretch the neck muscles.

2. Taking the head to the base of the tail to stretch the shoulders and back muscles.

3. Repeat in the opposite direction.

4. Tucking the chin into the neck to stretch the muscles on the back of the neck.

5. Elevating the head, pointing towards the sky, stretching the under neck and chest muscles.

6. A supported play bow to stretch the pelvis, lower spine and shoulders.

7. Extension of front legs and back legs, with supported balance.

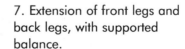

8. Not all dogs are comfortable in this position, but where the spine is supported on the floor, roll the dog slowly from one side to the other.

9. An advanced movement to stretch the tummy muscles, and pelvic muscles, lots of support needed.

GAME 4:2   # Everyday Exercise: STAND SIT   **LEVEL 1**

Exercise for:	
ALL AGE GROUPS	All dogs should be able to perform this movement with ease.
MOBILITY	Hip joints can benefit from appropriate daily repetition to build muscle strength. Mobility is improved in the older dog when performed slowly.
FLEXIBLE JOINTS	Sport exercises can significantly improve the speed of a sit, the set off from sitting and the accuracy of the sit. Dogs with weak hip joints can benefit from appropriate daily repetition.
JOINT STRENGTH	

PREVIOUS SKILLS
Sit, by cue or lure.

RESOURCES
Suitable food to stimulate, but not fixate the dog.

NATURAL PROGRAMME

Very young puppies, up to 5/6 months old will often sit naturally forward and backwards depending on the stimuli. A pup sitting behind a fence watching an activity with keen interest will often sit forwards. This is play-learning the movement of watching prey intently. The body completes the action of sitting (or lying down) with the minimal interference with the head, which can maintain a fixed watch on the prey. Sheepdogs will stand watching the sheep with a low head carriage, and move into a sit or a down without any discernable movement to the head.

Pups will often sit backward when pondering something, when the brain is puzzling over a new noise or situation.

You can capture either type of sit as they occur, mimic the prey stimulus with toys or free shaping puzzles.

PATTERN OF PROGRESS Steps of increasing criteria	CLICK to mark	REWARD location

JUNIOR PROGRAMME

1. Lure the opposing movements of going into a sit from standing and rising to a stand from sitting. Initially the dog can choose their style of action, ie: to step backward to sit (a back sit), or walk their rear legs forward to sit (forward sit).	For consistent completion of actions.	In outcome position, ie: the sit or stand.

If the dog is slow to rise from the sit, click for the sit, but lure to the stand with the open palm. This will inhibit over relaxation of the muscles after sitting and maintain tighter joints.

ADULT PROGRAMME

To encourage forward or backward sit, change the location of the lure to stimulate the desired movement. A forward sit for sit to heel, or present position in front is recommended
Similarly to control the rising action, whether the dog steps forward to the stand, (recommended for Show Dogs), or the rear feet walk backwards to rise (recommended for Obedience Competitions), will depend on the placement of the food for delivery, and lure to trigger the behaviour.

BACKWARD SIT - FORWARD STAND, lure with hand over skull, and move level hand over hips.	Consistent action.	Forward to step into the stand.
FORWARD SIT - BACKWARD STAND, lure with food close to nose, and other hand behind skull to prevent backward movement	Consistent action.	Food to sternum, to encourage rear feet to step backwards.

SPORTS PROGRAMME

Extending the forward sit/backward sit, forward stand, backward stand movements with luring will increase strength to the hip action and speed can be built.

Build movements in matching pairs only, ie forward stand with backward sit, and backward stand with forward sit.
ACCURACY AND ENDURANCE IN THE SIT

When in the sit, with your hand on the side of the dog, slightly push the dog off centre. Click for resistance and feed when back to the centred position. Begin with pressure at hip height and progress upwards to shoulder height. Slowly increase the pressure over several months and click the increase in resistance.

ELDERLY PROGRAMME

Always allow the speed of movement to be at the dog's choice. Let every movement be successful and rewarded.

ADD THE CUE

All the actions can be put onto final cues. Both the different sit and stand actions will have a different cues, a total of four cues.

Sitting is not just an outcome but often used as the preliminary for a range of quite different behaviours:

Sit: whilst I throw an article   Sit: whilst I walk to the first jump

Sit: in heel position waiting to set off   Sit: stay there whilst I put your lead on

The verbal cue "sit" can be used, but the contextual cues, of the article, the jump, the proximity, the location will add the type of sit. Consistency and understanding the collection of the four cues is the secret to consistent behaviour

GAME 4:3	**Everyday Exercise: STAND DOWN**	LEVEL 1

Exercise for:
AGES: ADULT, SPORTS
MOBILITY
STRENGTH
BALANCE

This movement should be the clean drop from standing to a lion down, and the clean lift from the down to the stand. All four legs must go into action at the same time for the spine to be maintained horizontal, not a sit and then a walk into the down.

This action takes considerable strength and flexibility. The two actions: can be performed without ANY movement of the feet, requiring all the joints of the legs to control the action.

Most dogs should be able to perform this movement with ease, but some may take several development sessions to build muscle strength.

Look for signs of weakness such as a quick drop and fast release of muscle control - you will hear a thud as the dog lands.

PREVIOUS SKILLS
Lion down.

RESOURCES
Suitable food to stimulate, but not fixate the dog.

PATTERN OF PROGRESS Steps of increasing criteria   CLICK to mark   REWARD location

ADULT PROGRAMME

1. Begin with the dog in a lion, or sphinx, down position. The dog must be equally balanced on either hip, with both front legs straight out. Lure the dog to a stand position by placing the offered food forwards of the dog at nose height.	Response to rise.	When standing.

It is easier to observe the correct action when the dog rises from the lion down to a clean stand. Ideally the feet should not move. This means the food should be drawn from the dog's nose in the down to where the dog will stand, a diagonally rising movement.
Observe this action carefully, and when the dog can rise with a clean action, move the hand in exactly the opposite direction to drop the dog backwards into a lion down.
Most easily trained when the dog stands across the front of you, at eye level, sit on the floor with the dog or place the dog on a table.

2. Observe this action carefully, and when the dog can rise with a clean action, move the hand in exactly the opposite direction to drop the dog backwards into a lion down.	Sinking backwards movement.	In the down, but do not allow relaxation.

SPORTS PROGRAMME

Great strength can be built with these movements taught as push-ups. The dog will drop with ease and speed, and be able to rise directly from the down and prepare for forward movement.

The dog must be fluid and relaxed in the adult programme and able to repeat 10 repetitions in each direction.

Do not feed in the down position it will relax the joints. Click in the down keeping the joints tight, poised for the fast lift to the food.

To develop the strong joint action, cue the drop movement, but click for the first dip and immediately lure with the reward back up to the stand.

Keep increasing the degree of the dip until the dog is fractionally off the floor. Do not repeat the extreme movement more than five times, cool down with adult programme, feeding in both stand and down.

ADD THE CUE

The drop action is likely to have a more instant response when cued from their standing position than the action from stand, into a sit then into a down.

Each action can have its own cue: "drop" from standing, "down" from sitting. Both actions are then kept separate giving a more accurate response from the dog.

GAME 4:4 | **Everyday Exercise: SIT BEG** | LEVEL 1

Exercise for:
AGES: NURSERY, OLDER
AGES: ADULT, SENIOR
MOBILITY
STRENGTH OF BACK
BALANCE

This is an excellent movement to tighten the pelvic muscles and strengthen the back muscles.

Pups under 5/6 months old and elderly dogs, should perform the nursery version of the exercise.

PREVIOUS SKILLS
Lion down, hand target

RESOURCES
Suitable food to stimulate, but not fixate the dog.

PATTERN OF PROGRESS Steps of increasing criteria   CLICK to mark   REWARD location

NURSERY BEG
This teaches a good hip and back balance and is an entirely natural move. When 6 - 8 week old pups are feeding from a standing bitch, the pups all beg with their front paws on the dam, and each other, for support.
Use a lure to mimic the behaviour and let the pups paws rest on you.

Seeking the balance point and then the maintenance.

In the beg whilst learning balance.
In the sit when opening the action.

TARGET BEG
1. Using a target stick, rise the dog from a balanced, square sit, so that their front feet just leave the ground. The target end needs to be above the dog's skull and slightly behind. A target hand can inhibit movement when you lean over the dog.

Rising to the target.

In the balanced sit.

2. Increase the action, moving the target further backwards, avoid too much height (see picture opposite)

Increased effort, but under control.

In the balanced sit.

3. Use the target stick to maintain the position, and develop duration to build strength.

Finding the balance point.

In the beg position.

PAW TO PALM BEG

For older dogs used to the action, ask for a "high five" paw to palm and click for the paw maintaining contact whilst in the sit.

Once comfortable, gently push the dog up into the beg position, maintain contact with the paw for support.

For older dogs or dogs with conformation that make this difficult to maintain, keep the contact with the paw when increasing duration.

SPORTS PROGRAMME

Once in an easily sustainable beg position teach the dog to go from a lion down to beg and back again. This builds exceptional strength.

Other movements of the paw can be added to the behaviour, such as wipe your face, and high five.

Notice how far back the dog's head is from the original sitting position. When using the target stick the movement must be backward and slightly up or the dog will try to jump.

See how the pelvis has moved forwards to balance the upper body.

ADD THE CUE

When the behaviour is fully established and strong, change from the target stick to a final cue.

GAME 4:5 | Everyday Exercise: DOWN SIT | LEVEL 1

Exercise for:
AGES: ADULT, SPORTS
MOBILITY
STRENGTH OF BACK
BALANCE

Sit to beg movements should be developed to build strength in the back muscles which enable a clean "jerk" movement from the down to the sit.

The conformation of some dogs will restrict their rising speed. Watch the natural movement of the dog rising in uncued, everyday situations.

Regular training of this movement will improve back strength and affect the style of the movement.

PREVIOUS SKILLS
Sit to beg strength.

RESOURCES
Suitable food to stimulate, but not fixate the dog. Target stick or toy.

PATTERN OF PROGRESS Steps of increasing criteria | **CLICK to mark** | **REWARD location**

PATTERN OF PROGRESS	CLICK to mark	REWARD location
1. Begin with the dog in a clean, balanced sit. The hips must be equally balanced. Lure, or target into a snap down position, look for speed and avoid the "walk down". Make sure the lure point is forward and down to the final placement of the head.	The speedy "snap" to the lion down.	Lure up to the sit to feed.

Make sure the click in the down position does not cue a settled movement. The dog's muscles must be held tense ready for the quick return to the sitting position.

VARIATIONS

	CLICK to mark	REWARD location
Build the dog with lure, click and lift repetitions. Extra strength can then be developed with a stronger motivator after the click - ie: a toss of the food or toy that can be caught with a quick rise to the sit.	The speedy "snap" to the lion down.	Toss food or toy to catch in the sit position.

ADD THE CUE

Remember the cue for the movement of a down to a sit is NOT "sit".
The muscle collection is entirely different and requires a unique cue.

GAME 4:6

Everyday Exercise: DOWN SETTLE

LEVEL 1

Exercise for:
ALL AGE GROUPS
RELAXED POSITION
FLEXIBLE HIP JOINTS
FLEXIBILITY OF SPINE

This exercise is particularly good for hip mobility. When teaching a novice dog, a preference or weakness of either side will become apparent.

Observe the dog in their natural environment when not training and keep a record of their preferred hip to settle onto. Ensure that training balances both sides equally if there is a preference.

PREVIOUS SKILLS
Down position.

RESOURCES
Suitable food to stimulate, but not fixate the dog.

PATTERN OF PROGRESS Steps of increasing criteria	CLICK to mark	REWARD location
1. Begin with the lion down, with both hips equally balanced and the front weight of the dog on their elbows. Lure the dog's head to their right and downward, towards their right back foot.	As soon as the hips shift to one side.	In the settled position.
2. Move back to the lion position by pulling the next lure forwards in front of the dog, where their front feet will be.	As soon as the hips move to lion position.	In the lion position.

Lure the dog to settle on the left side.
Rotate through all three positions: Lion, settle to right, lion, settle to the left

| | |
--- | --- | ---
3. A maintained settled position can be taught by rewarding always in position. | Soft click (relax) for position. | In the settle, near back foot to maintain relaxed posture.

ADD THE CUE

Both left and right settle can be given independent cues.

To teach a settle choice, (ie: settle yourself as you will) use a hand signal, (as the lure signal), and place the dog to settle so that it can maintain a good view of pertinent activities.

GAME 4:7 — Everyday Exercise: **CIRCLE** — LEVEL 1

Exercise for:
ALL AGE GROUPS
MOBILITY OF SPINE
STRENGTH OF BACK
BALANCE

This exercise is exceptionally good for mobility of the spine and developing balance through turns.

It can be taught equally to the Nursery, Junior and Older, Elderly groups with gentle progress and developed for the Adult Sports to build strength.

Always maintain the lure with the head in a naturally carried position, not raised. Make sure the Sports training does not over speed.

PREVIOUS SKILLS
None.

RESOURCES
Suitable food to stimulate, but not fixate the dog. Target stick or toy.

PATTERN OF PROGRESS Steps of increasing criteria

PATTERN OF PROGRESS Steps of increasing criteria	CLICK to mark	REWARD location
1. Begin with the dog standing with their side close to your legs. Lure the head away in a circle, aiming the head towards the base of the dog's tail.	Following the lure.	Each step of the way around the circle.
2. Progress in small increments around the circle, making sure the spine maintains an equal curvature.	Following the lure.	Each step of the way around the circle.
3. Gradually increase the section of the circle completed before the visual click, until the full circuit is achieved.	The furthest point away.	When standing ready for the next circle.
4. Teach circles in both directions. Very often one side is easier for the dog than the other, include a balancing selection in your programme to equal the mobility.		

For long backed dogs, or dogs that are not comfortable with the degree of leaning a hand lure would enforce, use a target stick.

SPORTS PROGRAMME

Strength can be built through greater motivation to follow a toy around the circle. Make sure the dog does not lose the curvature of the spine as speed increases, or moves away from the same location.

Using the corner of a room or fencing can ensure the dog maintains a healthy shape through repetitions.

Using a tug with the dog holding onto it, can increase the curvature. Always ensure the dog's head is level or below their natural carriage. Avoid flipping the dog with pressure on the neck.

ADD THE CUE
Both left and right circles can be given independent cues or modifier cues.

GAME 4:8 — Everyday Exercise: BOW — LEVEL 1

Exercise for:
ALL AGE GROUPS
MOBILITY OF SPINE
STRENGTH OF BACK
BALANCE

PREVIOUS SKILLS
None.

The bow, originated from the natural play bow, or invitation to play, moves the spine through an "S" shape on the vertical plane.

It stretches the muscles up the back of the dog's back legs (similar to a human touching their toes), and stretches the upper back in the opposing direction with a good curve to the neck.

Holding the position also opens the hip joints and pelvic muscles.

Luring this position is quite skilled. The correct direction is triggering a movement between the dog taking a step backwards and the dog going into a drop. A diagonal direction from the dog's nose, downward to a point just behind their front feet is required.

RESOURCES
Suitable food to stimulate, but not fixate the dog. Target stick or toy.

PATTERN OF PROGRESS Steps of increasing criteria

	PATTERN OF PROGRESS	CLICK to mark	REWARD location
1.	With the dog standing facing you, lure the initial dip of the head and shoulders. You may need to kneel or sit on the floor with the dog.	The lowest point in the dip.	Standing up in the starting position.
2.	Keep progressing the degree of dip maintaining a fluent movement. The feet should remain stationary and the hips upright.	The lowest point in the dip.	Standing up in the starting position.
3.	Lure through to the elbows touching the floor, allow the dog to rest in this position with the hips in the air.	Elbows on the floor, hips in the air.	Standing up in the starting position.

To teach the dog to hold this position some initial discomfort may force the dog to drop their hips to a down position. Gently place your hand in front of their knee to keep it upright. Let the muscles up the back of the legs stretch gently.

SPORTS PROGRAMME

Build additional strength by asking the dog to move from a lion down position UP into a bow, maintaining the chest on the floor.

Begin in the down position and lure forwards very slightly along the floor. The rear will rise to change the dog's point of balance, you can also assist with a slight touch to the front of the dog's knee to trigger a back step of the rear legs.

Cute cue: Kiss my Ass!

ADD THE CUE

Very often the word "bow" is confusing for the dog if the cue "down" is also in their repertoire. Suggestions are "take a bow" or "bend".

GAME 4:9 — Everyday Exercise: **FLAT ROLL** — LEVEL 1

Exercise for:
ALL AGE GROUPS
MOBILITY OF SPINE
STRENGTH OF BACK
RELAXATION

The completed exercise at speed would look like a roll over, but by teaching each position a greater fitness and mobility benefit can be achieved.

Some elderly dogs, and the conformation of some dogs may make lying upside down uncomfortable.

PREVIOUS SKILLS
Lure down to settle.
Rewards with stroking.

RESOURCES
Suitable food to stimulate, but not fixate the dog.

PATTERN OF PROGRESS Steps of increasing criteria	CLICK to mark	REWARD location
1. Begin with the dog in the Settled Down. Take the lure toward the foot of the upper most hip, making an exaggerated "C" shape.	The increased settled position.	In the position if it is comfortably held.
2. In this position if the right hip is upper most, the left elbow is supporting much of the weight of the dog's front end. Take the lure from the foot directly up the dog's back towards their spine to encourage the weight shift onto the left shoulder.	The weight onto the shoulder.	Back in the above settled position.
3. Once comfortable and responsive to this position, begin to feed in position which should encourage the dog to lie flat to the floor.	Lying flat.	Lying flat, or back in settled position to practice the move.
4. From the flat position, move the lure to take the dog's head towards the upper most elbow and keep moving toward the shoulders until the dog is lying on its back.	Response to movement and shifting weight.	Lying flat, unless safe to feed upside down.
5. Once lying upside down lure the dog to complete the roll to the opposite lying flat. Lure both ways to ensure equal muscle effort.	Rolling out.	In the flat position.

If the dog has difficulty maintaining the upside down position, a paw touch with the leg pointing upwards to your hand can help the balance, or gentle tummy stroking to relax the muscles.

SPORTS PROGRAMME

Teaching a "speed roll" will increase all the muscles of the mid section. Be very carefully to only let the speed commence after the dog is in a clean down position and paused, before the speed roll and back into a standing position. A fast dog can begin the rolling process too soon if cued from standing and land on their shoulder.

Always teach both directions.

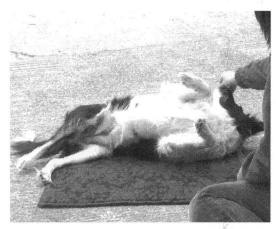

ADD THE CUE

Both roll directions can be given independent cues or modifier cues.

| GAME 4:10 | **Flexi-gility: BALANCE** | LEVEL 1 |

Developing:
SELF CONTROL
CO-ORDINATION
CONFIDENCE
LEAD WALKING SKILLS

PREVIOUS SKILLS
Sit, down, stop, turn around.

Most dogs will only learn muscle movement to meet their everyday requirements. In young puppies under 20 weeks, developing co-ordination and balance is also developing additional parts of the brain. For older dogs over 1 year this exercises need to use existing skills and adapt them rather than develop new skills.

ALWAYS allow puppy or dog to make free choices when exploring equipment, and allow frequent rest on the ground.

Raise the criteria only on a demonstration of confidence. At no time lure the learner to make progress, exploration is always at their choice, demonstrating confidence in the situation, themselves and their learning.

RESOURCES
Level, very stable, planks raised approx 20-30cm, or 8 - 12". Placed side by side for large dogs making a wider plank, at "T" junctions and angles. Increasing difficult as the learning progresses with height and slopes.

PATTERN OF PROGRESS Steps of increasing criteria

PATTERN OF PROGRESS	CLICK to mark	REWARD location
1. Teach the dog to approach and climb onto the plank. Place yourself the opposite side of the plank. Reward approach and exploration. Keep repeating this approach stage until the dog is returning keen and confident and ready to make the first paw contact.	Approach, and contact.	Feed on the ground, to allow repetition of approach.
2. Reward the learner for placing front paws onto plank, from just a light touch through to full weight on both feet.	Touch and then weight transfer.	Feed on the ground, to allow repetition of contact.
3. Step back away from the plank, making sure the dog has room to step forward towards you, onto the plank with back legs.	Back legs climbing on.	Feed on plank by front feet*.
4. Turn to face left or right, with your shoulder nearest the plank indicating a cue to walk by your side.	Turning with co-ordination in the same direction	Feed on plank by front feet*.

* When rewarding the position on the equipment make sure the food is placed on the plank, and can be eaten without additional movement. Feeding direct to the dog's mouth can cause them to stumble and lose balance. Focus with the plank needs to be maintained.

VARIATIONS

Build patterns with a series of level planks that encourage left and right turns, full about turns and changes of direction.

Only reward the dog responding to your shoulder cues for directional changes.

Include small obstacles for the dog to step over whilst maintaining a position at your side. Small bricks, poles and hoops.

Change the width of the planks, dependent on the dog's size.

Teach changing heights, stepping up to a higher level, moving under a fly-over plank and up and down slopes.

For dogs that find it difficult to concentrate in proximity of other dogs, once they have achieved a good level of self confidence on the planks introduce another dog working near by.

ADD THE CUE

The equipment is its own cue. Dogs should only move along the planks level with you and in the same direction. This is teaching the dog to multi-task. They will concentrate on the equipment and maintain self control to stay moving at your speed, match changes of direction and pauses.

Your shoulder movements are the directional cues.

GAME 4:11	**Flexi-gility: SURFACES**	LEVEL 1

Developing: EXPERIENCE CO-ORDINATION BALANCE CONFIDENCE	Walking over a range of surfaces develops excellent co-ordination skills and gives the dogs experiences that build self confidence. Pups under 20 weeks especially benefit with this experiential learning. Surfaces need to develop balance, altered movement and can be useful if used as part of the lead walking training. Where possible feed from the surface without any luring.
PREVIOUS SKILLS Flexi-gility balance.	**RESOURCES** Range of surfaces.

Young pups can enjoy group learning with a handful of pups exploring together. Place treats on the different surfaces and allow free grazing.
Adults may be more comfortable learning individually.

PATTERN OF PROGRESS Steps of increasing criteria	CLICK to mark	REWARD location
1. Lead controlled walking on new surfaces can teach self control and multi tasking. Always click when the dog looks at new surfaces, makes decisions, and makes contact.	Confident but not panicky, moves.	From hand or the surface if possible.
LARGE BOARDS. Most boards are not flat, they usually warp slightly. Begin with the board flat to the floor, and then raise one corner with a small stone or book.		A new texture on the pads, and learning to react to a change of balance.
PAINTED FLOORS. Some dogs respond with tension in the feet and make transition across the surface even harder. Reward for the relaxation of the foot, place islands of safety (mats) in close proximity, expanding the gaps when confidence develops.		A solid surface with low friction.
BUBBLE WRAP OR CELLOPHANE. This will give a peculiar experience with the popping bubbles and the surface sticking to the paws. The material is likely to shift with the dog's progress.		Slightly tacky and moving.
WIGGLY TIN. (Sheets of corrugated iron). Everything about this surface will warn the dog to take care. Not only is the surface always uneven, it is very likely to wobble at the same time, and maybe slippery.		Metal, uneven and wobbly.

BRIDGES. Ideally a familiar surface, that may have some movement, and a sense of crossing over a void. Walking over London Bridge is not the same as a rope walk over a deep canyon. Build the experiences slowly, look for opportunities as you travel around.

Walking over a void.

PICK-A-STICKS. Take a series of poles or light sticks and strew than on the floor in a random pattern. As the dog moves over the poles, their feet will make contact, move the poles, trip on the poles etc.

Negotiating on variable surface, contact with legs.

NETTING OR FENCING. Lay a roll of fencing or netting on the floor. This will give a varied sensation. Depending on the type of fencing, random bricks can be placed underneath to change the height.

Negotiating an variable surface, contact with legs.

NATURE'S FLOORING. Look for natural surfaces that offer learning experiences:
Very shallow running water, puddles, mud, shallow waves,

Wet grass, especially tall wet grass

Tall grasses over the dog's head

Piles of leaves, fresh snow, sand, pebbles

Look for surfaces with tactile sensations, demanding balance, contact with the legs.

TOUCH SENSATIONS. Place a table cloth, or long sheet, over a table with the sides draping about half way down. The pups can enter from one end and experience the sensation of a non-contacting tunnel, or enter from the sides and brush under the table cloth. As confidences develops drop the cloth lower so that the dog needs to push against the cloth to progress (or get that piece of sausage).
Additional "danglers" can be draped, such as dog leads, where the ends are weighted and give different sensations.

Contact sensations around the body. Pushing through barriers.

ADD THE CUE

The cue for Confidence, Self Control and multi-tasking is the lead and proximity by your side.

Through the Flexi-gility exercises the dog will learn that they can always trust your judgement, keep them safe and trying out new things will be rewarded.

GAME 4:12	Flexi-gility: CAVALETTI	LEVEL 1

Developing:
RHYTHMIC TROTTING
CONCENTRATION
MUSCLE TONE

Cavaletti movement requires the dog to trot in a fixed rhythm set by the gap between the poles

Adjusting the width demands a change in momentum:

> A narrower gap and the poles raised (by an height equal to the gap reduction) cause a pulling back of momentum.

> A wider gap, ground level poles, causes a forward drive in momentum.

PREVIOUS SKILLS

Moving from target A to Target B (3:11 page 46)

RESOURCES

Set of cavaletti poles, with height variable from ground level to just above the stop pad, with adjustable gaps between poles.

Two teachers, or target mats.

PATTERN OF PROGRESS Steps of increasing criteria	CLICK to mark	REWARD location
1. Set the cavaletti markers (not the poles) out as a channel for the dog to run through as they go from A to B, (where A & B are teachers or target mats at the end)	Leaving one target.	Arriving at other target
2. Place 5 poles out at the dog's nursery distance. Place 4 pieces of easily visible food, one piece centrally between the poles. Let the dog follow and eat as the food is placed, with a final piece at the end target. Repeat several times.	(Stepping over each pole.) The behaviour is self rewarding, a click is not necessary.	From the placed food.
3. Reduce the food so that only one piece remains centrally between pole 2 and 3. Then complete as above, ensuring the dog moves out of the Cavalettis, turns around, and sets up for a correct approach	Approaching poles.	From piece in the poles, and then end target.
4. Remove food from the poles. Look for trotting action.	The trot.	At the target.
5. Shape a balanced, confident action, with correct drive to avoid hitting poles.	Balanced movement	At the target.
For dogs that are slow to begin trotting:	As the dog begins the action.	
For dogs that vary in action:	On the correct action	

If the dog races the poles, move the targets closer to the last poles. If the dog is very slow, move the targets further apart. Always allow enough gap for the dog to find the action before starting on the poles.

JUNIOR PROGRAMME

NURSERY GAP: The distance from the dog's front toes to back toes.

OPTIMUM GAP: 20 cm above Nursery gap for a medium sized dog.

This must be adjusted depending on the action of the dog. Some dogs of the same size have short gaits, others have significant ground reaching gaits. Look for a level topline (neck to hips) that is balanced with a rhythmic movement.

SPORTS PROGRAMME

BUILDING STAMINA

Puppies can begin cavaletti work when they demonstrate sustained trotting in a natural environment without external stimulation, ie. pottering around the garden. Keep the duration very low with no more than 4 repetitions* and ensure a change in action/activity before another repetition*.

Adult dogs should rest for 2 minutes, after every 5 set of repetitions. The rest should be a controlled walk, not lying down or trotting, but keeping the muscles warm but not under exertion. At the end of the session the dogs should be walked for 3-5 minutes to cool down. Always ensure the dog is not so over heated that they need to flop down.

For Adult (Sports) Dogs:

    1. Warm up: 5 repetitions of 5 poles at Optimum gap

    2. Session 1 - 5   5 repetitions of 9 poles at Optimum gap

    3. Sessions 6 - 10   10 repetitions of 9 poles at Optimum gap

    4. Sessions 11-15   15 repetitions of 9 poles at Optimum gap (and weekly maintenance)

*REPETITION this is the transition from Station A to B and back to A, ie the dog will make 2 transitions of the poles for one repetition.

BUILDING STRENGTH

Dogs should have completed the stamina development up to maintenance level before these exercises.

    a) Stretch: increase pole gap by 10% (max of 15%), no more than 5 repetitions.

    b) Lift: reduce pole gap (from optimum) by 10cm, increase height 20cm, no more than 5 repetitions.

Follow both these exercises with 5 repetitions of 9 poles at Optimum gap, and then the usual walk down to cool.

Both exercises should show some degree of extra effort from the dog, but not so much that the dog struggles to complete the sets.

ADD THE CUE

Temporary Cue: Target or teacher. Final Cue: "Go to" / "Station" in conjunction with directional cue (ie: to which target) from trainer's body language.

| GAME 4:13 | Flexi-gility: FOLLOW | LEVEL 2 |

Developing:
VARIOUS GAITS
CONCENTRATION
MUSCLE TONE

PREVIOUS SKILLS
Following a moving target.

The dog will need a very good foundation in touching a moving target (page 37).

Concentration should be easily maintained and of some duration.

Various gaiting actions can be taught by varying:

the speed of the moving target

the angle of the dog's head when following the target

the pattern of the movement, on the curve

Do not use a "follow me" target end for backing away movement.

RESOURCES

Target stick with easily visible end target, extendible beyond arm's length.

Even work surface of good under foot purchase: carpet, short grass etc.

PATTERN OF PROGRESS Steps of increasing criteria	CLICK to mark	REWARD location
1. Warm up the dog with several short (5-8 seconds) of following the eye level target in an easy trot. Gain familiarity and security with the surface and the environment. Move the dog in a large race track pattern in both directions.	Good focus on target and relaxed, rhythmic action.	Toss beyond target end, do NOT bring the dog to you for reward.
WALK ON, SLOW WALK. Slow the movement of the target stick, tuck the dog's head slightly lower than normal.	Easy, balance with self control.	Beyond target end.
TROT UP, COLLECTED TROT. Toss a treat at some distance and set the dog up to return towards you with some momentum, preferably a controlled trot. Bring onto the target, initially with a level top line. To collect the action, move the dog's point of balance further back by slightly raising the target end. As the dog's head tips up, reduce speed and allow the front end to elevate slightly.	The developing action, with increasing criteria for exaggerated or sustained movement with good momentum.	Beyond target end.

Your own movement can hinder or help the dog. Avoid teaching a highly animated action when you are moving slowly and vice versa.

ADULT PROGRAMME

Different gaits can be achieved by changing the height of the target end, and the speed over the floor.

The result will vary from dog to dog, and even within the same breed. Conformation and structure play a large part in the outcome, and training can only enhance or exaggerate the existing movement.

All movements can be put on cue, actions can be trained for the Show ring, for Obedience Heelwork or for Freestyle. A creep can be taught with the target stick at floor level and the dog commencing in the down (but only for dogs who exhibit this behaviour naturally).

For a sustained action, develop muscle strength by changing the surface to one with less resistance, such as sand.

Tug games will also help build the supporting body strength.

focal point forward

focal point upward

ADD THE CUE

The target end is the temporary cue and action can be transferred to a new cue when training is completed.

The Action Cue can be associated with a Location Cue (on my left side), or a Target Cue (trot towards the judge)

GAME 4:14	Flexi-gility: BACKING	LEVEL 2

Developing:
ALL AGES
BACK LEG MOVEMENT
SELF CONFIDENCE
SELF CONTROL
SPATIAL AWARENESS

PREVIOUS SKILLS

Front feet to target mat.
(3:4 page 34).

Backing movements, at the walk, trot or bounce, are a demonstration of excellent physical mobility, a sense of spatial awareness (where they are in relation to the teacher or other objects). It can be taught either:

> as a movement

> as an outcome of moving to a target

Teaching as a movement is a free shape behaviour where the dog steps backwards. A sounder movement is achieved by marking the reaching back of the back legs, not the front legs, as this movement initiated by front legs tends to end in a hunched, cramped posture.

Teaching contact with a target develops movement and spatial awareness, and can be the foundation learning for working at a distance.

RESOURCES

Target mat or surface change.

PATTERN OF PROGRESS Steps of increasing criteria   CLICK to mark   REWARD location

	CLICK to mark	REWARD location
1. Refresh the dog with the target mat, where the front feet are on the mat, and the dog is standing in front of you facing you. Sit in a chair or on the floor to maintain a level eye contact.	Solid position on the mat.	Standing on the mat, alternated with food tossed behind the dog.

Standing on the mat should be reinforced as a secure place to be, with the dog skilled in finding this position by walking onto the mat towards you. Movement back to the mat will be back chained.

	CLICK to mark	REWARD location
2. Lure the dog from standing on the mat approx 5cm, 2" forwards to feed. At least one front foot should leave the mat. Wait for the dog to step back to their historically reinforced location, on the mat.	Backing movement.	Lure the dog forward approx 5cm, 2". Feed at mouth level or lower.
3. Very, very gradually increase the gap between the mat and reward location. Only increase with your movement away from the dog, not moving the mat away from you.	Arriving on mat.	Several repetitions at each distance forwards.

If the dog turns away from you to step onto the mat, the lure gap has increased too quickly. Start again, click several backing movements, before increasing the criteria to movement THEN contact with the mat.

SPORTS PROGRAMME

Increase distance until a balanced fluid movement is achieved.

To build fluid movement without stress, cue the dog to reverse towards the mat, and when moving comfortably follow the dog until the mat is reached. For example, if the dog walks backward to 2m, 6ft, with you standing stationary, begin at a gap of 3m, 9ft, for the mat. Cue the dog to begin, as they approach the 2m, 6ft point, start to follow the dog, moving together the last metre onto the mat. The gap between you should not decrease. By following (mimicking) the dog you reinforce the movement, and avoid additional stress that the increasing distance can cause. Avoid closing onto the dog as this adds pressure and can distort the movement.

Climbing backwards up a staircase is a high level oppositional exercise. Begin with the mat on the top level of the staircase, lure the dog to step down one step. Click for recovery of the top step. Build slowly with several repetitions at each point. The front feet will acquired the behaviour fairly rapidly, the back legs become a new behaviour and may take some development.

Backing at your side or towards you (tail first), can be taught by transferring your location relevant to the mat.

Begin a reasonable distance, 3m/9ft, from the mat and vary your location relevant to the dog. Feed in exactly the same spot each time, a reward station would be useful.Generalise the movement to a wide variation in your location until you can stand anywhere relevant to the dog or mat and the behaviour maintains the standard.

You can then teach synchronised or parallel movement.

Teaching the dog to walk backwards in a circle is taught with a small circular pen that influences the shape of the backing. Try to click for the inside back leg stepping towards the centre of the circle as this is the repetitive movement that causes the line to curve.

ADD THE CUE

If you want to be able to cue this behaviour irrelevant to your location a verbal cue needs to be added. The dog should not need to look at you for the cue as very often they are looking away from you.

| GAME 4:15 | **Flexi-gility: SIDE STEPPING** | LEVEL 2 |

Developing:

ALL AGES

BACK LEG MOVEMENT

SELF AWARENESS

SPATIAL AWARENESS

Side, or lateral, movements are invaluable exercises for physical flexibility and enhances a whole range of movements.

Closely watch your own dog around its natural environment and analyse how the dog moves its hips to one side. If the dog moves to its left, it will either step with the back left leg and close the gap with back right leg, or cross the back right leg over the back left leg, which then completes the move with a step to the left.

Teaching the dog's natural movement will avoid stress and result in speedier learning.

PREVIOUS SKILLS

Front feet to target mat. (3:4 page 34).

Rehearse your movements before teaching the dog.

RESOURCES

More than two target mats.

PATTERN OF PROGRESS Steps of increasing criteria   CLICK to mark   REWARD location

Stand facing your dog approximately one stride apart with the dog's front feet on the target mat. Regard the layout as if the mat is the centre of a clock, the dog's front feet stand in the centre, your feet are at 6 o'clock, and the dog's back feet are at 12 o'clock.

#	Steps of increasing criteria	CLICK to mark	REWARD location
1.	Build a reinforcement history of this position and relative location to you. Vary the reward location with food tossed beyond 12 o'clock and the dog returning to their "spot".	Standing on mat in 12 o'clock position.	On the mat and sometimes beyond.
2.	Holding your hands together at waist height and still facing the centre of the clock, take several small side steps towards 9 o'clock.	The dog reflecting your movement to 3 o'clock.	On the mat at your opposite point.
3.	Build a strong movement in both directions to at least half a clock, or 180°. Look for increasingly fluid movement and observe the back leg stride pattern. (Movement 1)	The movement arriving to the median line.	On the mat at your opposite point.
4.	Open with Movement 1 and as the dog arrives to the median point (6 o'clock) side step to your left (Movement 2). Use the momentum from Movement 1 and the front legs stimulus to the second mat.	The movement arriving to the median line.	On the mat at your opposite point.
5.	Build fluency and discriminate for maintenance of a straight back. Avoid reinforcing a front leg / back leg disjointed movement.	Synchronised movement of front and back legs.	At your opposite point.

Movement 1

dog rotates with steps to their right with back feet

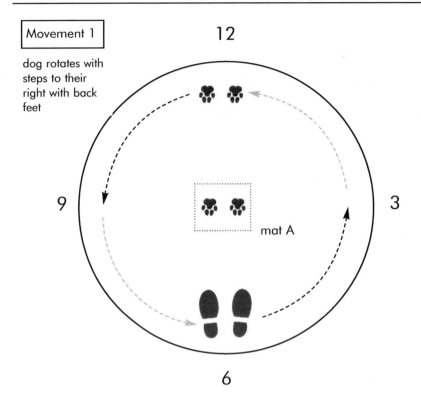

Movement 2

dog rotates and then steps to their right with front AND back feet

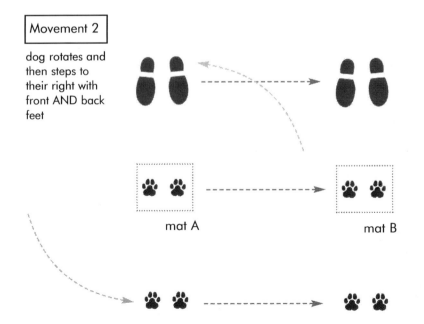

Practise in both directions. It is natural for the dog to be more comfortable in one direction than the other. Ensure more practise on the less comfortable side.

ADD THE CUE

The cue evolves from the learning experience. Dogs are expert at reading slight changes in balance that result in movement. As your leg makes the initial step in Movement 1 your matching shoulder will dip slightly.

By dipping the shoulder just prior to the step the dog can respond with synchronised movement.

If you want to use this cue to move in any other position, such as heel positions, then add a verbal cue for each direction or use modifier cues.

GAME 4:16 | Flexi-gility: SPRING JUMP | LEVEL 2

Developing:
AGES: JUNIOR, ADULT
JUMP SKILLS
OBSTACLE AWARENESS
MUSCLE TONE

PREVIOUS SKILLS
Flick Click.
Nose target to hand.
Rehearse the actions before teaching.

All dogs should learn carefully structured jumping skills. If left to their own learning it is natural for a dog to place their feet on the jump to get across it. Nature did not design dogs to jump blind to an unseen landing spot.

This natural jump combined with unsteady jumps, ie: poles or wire fences, results in an unhealthy, cramped jump. Healthy jumps are clean arcs where the front legs stretch forwards, the rear legs stretch out behind and the dogs spine is slightly arched. The power comes from the rear legs.

A spring jump is a push off the ground and land in the same spot. Very often the front and back legs leave the ground together. Lambs are expert at this. The power comes from the feet.

Jumping injuries occur because of unsuitable surfaces where the lack of purchase causes a poor take off or landing impact is too hard or slippery. All growth height must be completed before landing impact is introduced, although low level jumps can teach co-ordination.

RESOURCES
Hula hoop, light jump pole. Easily visible, bouncy treats

PATTERN OF PROGRESS Steps of increasing criteria   CLICK to mark   REWARD location

SPRING JUMP

Steps	CLICK to mark	REWARD location
1. Begin with dog standing in front and you kneeling on the floor. With the pole in your right hand, hold it at floor level on the dog's right. With your left hand offer the food out to your left and slightly behind you.	As the dog side steps over the pole.	To reset the dog standing in front on the other side of the pole.
2. Build step over confidence and muscle action until the dog offers a slight spring to the movement. Then begin to raise the pole very slightly.	As the dog side steps over the pole with a small spring.	To reset the dog standing in front on the other side of the pole.
3. Develop a fluid side spring action with the pole no higher than the dog's elbow. Then move the pole in the opposite direction as the dog springs up. You are trying to encourage a spring on the spot, therefore the pole must be moved out of the landing spot.	Spring on the spot with moving pole.	To reset the dog standing in front.

To transfer this behaviour when you are standing, thread a rope through the pole (pipe). Tie one end to a point at waist height and step away so that the pole can swing freely like a skipping rope.

PATTERN OF PROGRESS Steps of increasing criteria	CLICK to mark	REWARD location

CLEAN JUMP

1. With the hula hoop in your right hand, toss a opening treat away to your right to set the dog up to approach the hoop (1). Offer the lure to the dog to go through the hoop at ground level from your right to left. | Flick the wrist as the dog focuses on the approach to the hoop. | Toss the food to maintain the dog's forward movement. |

As the dog goes to collect their reward, rotate on the spot 180° and lure through the hoop again with your left hand. Throw the food a suitable distance to allow the dog to prepare before they go through the hoop.

2. Gradually increase in height, until a jumping action is triggered. Change hands with the hoop, and teach both directions so the dog is coming towards you for a treat thrown behind. | Clean, jump action. | Toss further away when raising the height. |

The hoop can be transferred as a jump target to other objects, and is excellent for teaching generalised body language to jumping actions.

opening treat

treat

ADD THE CUE

A verbal cue (unique to this particular spring movement) or hand action is needed to allow the jumping pole to be removed.

GAME 4:17   Sports Exercise: TUGGERS   LEVEL 2

Developing:
AGES: SPORTS ADULT
CONCENTRATION
MUSCLE TONE LEGS &
   BACK

These exercises are perfect for building good muscles tone, strength and flexibility. (I have also developed tremendous upper arms, twisted my neck regularly and wonder why my back is sore. Remember to keep your back straight, let your body weight be your strength, not the muscles in your arms or hands, and enjoy it as much as possible.)

The dog must be keen to tug, strength of bite is irrelevant, but the hold must be maintained.

Always make sure the dog goes through a proper warm up and cool down for these exercises.

PREVIOUS SKILLS
Tugging on toy.
Safety rules learned.

RESOURCES
Long tug, soft material slightly stretchy, good handle. Non slip surface.

PATTERN OF PROGRESS Steps of increasing criteria	CLICK to mark	REWARD location
1. Open with a balanced tug game. (page 132). Let the dog begin to increase rate of winning, with more releases or letting them pull you along.	Winning strength.	With extra ragging still on tug, or release for a break.
2. When the dog pulls in a head low position, follow the dog, or let the dog think they are winning. Try to keep the dog low, looking for contraction to the back muscles (nearly to the play bow) and the back legs spread for a good purchase.	Success in the pull, initially to communicate good action, then randomly.	Random release. (to allow you and the dog to shake out the muscles).
3. Once the dog has completed the above exercises, begin to lift the front legs of the dog from the ground, only very small amounts, and complete the same movement. Use common sense, if the dog is too tall or heavy for your height, this exercise can be passed over.	Same movement without front feet.	Frequent release, you'll need it.
4. From step 3, begin to pull the dog forwards, again without the front feet on the floor. This may be easier with the dog at your side and both progress together. If the dog is over strong in the sink-pull action, release the toy and ignore the dog, they need to be co-operative in this game.	Forward movement without front feet.	Frequent release.

Develop the side stepping movement of the back feet with similar pattern of progress.

Begin with the dog in front and a raised head tug, bounce the dog a small amount and rotate on the spot at the same time. Encourage the dog to start side stepping, rather than bouncing. You can significantly improve the back leg action for lateral work.

Make sure you work in both directions, and progress to back legs only when initial strength is developed.

ADD THE CUE

A specific cue for this behaviour is not necessary. The dog will learn the movements from your body language.

5 GAMES with the Sausage

Food games are probably the closest play ground where we can mimic nature's intent. Although playing with our food is frowned upon at the dinner table, for the dog it is a natural opportunity for interaction, since we manage 99% of their food supply. (And you don't want to know where the other 1% comes from). From a simple "where's your dinner?", that you have taken time to hide in the garden or the house, the focus and drive associated with eating can be transferred into our training sessions. Food, or the scent of food, becomes the cue to concentrate, anticipate and practise self control, all elements we want in the lessons. Rather akin to a children's classroom in a supermarket. Either a disaster for the learners without self control, or exciting and stimulating for those with self control.

During most of these games the presence or activity of the food will stimulate a specific behaviour. This is very often unique to these circumstances. The key to be able to use these behaviours and transfer food to the reward rather than the stimulus is the process of preceding with the new cue:

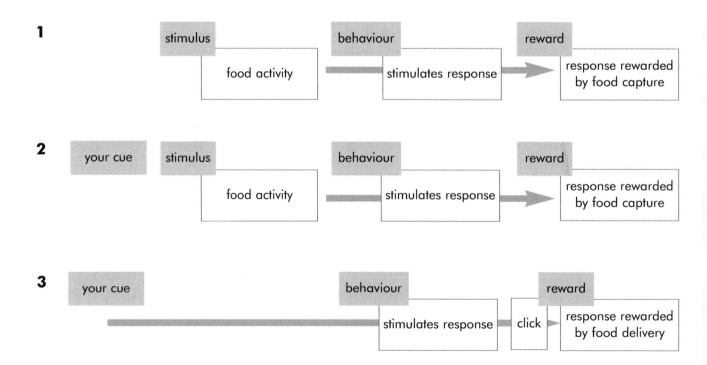

SAUSAGE OR CHEESE BALLS

The content of your food stimulus is not relevant, except that it must:

◆ be sufficiently motivating to keep the dog's attention

◆ be worth running for

◆ bounce in a most attractive and tantalising way

◆ be easily seen, followed and found

Half inch (1cm) portions of hot dogs, or hot dog "balls" (I'm sure these were invented for dogs), cubes or balls of cheese about the same size are ideal. When they are thrown they should not break into smaller pieces, but be easily handled and seen.

These games are not suitable for grassed surfaces, but similar games can be played with the toys for dogs that have a good retrieve.

SKILLS

You will need to be able to throw. Sure, everyone can throw. Hah! In my extensive experience in taking classes I have seen a dumbbell land on top of a car, a ball on a rope stuck up in a tree, a sausage added to a cup of tea.

Before you start to play structured games with the dog, practise tossing food to the dog and letting them run after it to capture. This is not mid air capture, but along the ground.

The ideal action is a knee bending under arm bowling throw. Crown green bowls, boules, ten pin bowl, skittles etc. all have a similar movement, where the ball is rolled along the ground, starting low to the ground. The bowling arm always follows through the action to appear to be maintaining the momentum of the ball after it is thrown. This is an excellent cue to the dog should they not see where the food has gone, your hand should be pointing straight at it.

the underarm bowling throw
with follow through

the frisbee throw:

the darts throw:

GAME 5:1 | WATCH THE MOUSE | LEVEL 1

Developing:
HIGH DEGREE OF FOCUS
INTERACTION

This is one of nature's best games.

Should your dog chase a mouse / rabbit which disappears down a hole, the dog will invest a serious amount of time watching that hole. Most mice are not stupid enough to poke their nose out of a hole stinking of dog breath, but the dog doesn't know that.

A captured behaviour from a strongly instinctive behaviour will develop very quickly and be easily transferable to a range of situations.

PREVIOUS SKILLS
Quick hand skills.

RESOURCES
Sausage or cheese balls.

PATTERN OF PROGRESS Steps of increasing criteria | mark | REWARD location

1. Sit on the floor with the dog in front of you, facing you. Take a food ball and place it on the floor between you. Keep your hand over the ball to prevent the dog from self rewarding.	No click. Just remove your hand when the dog is watching, and keeping still.	Dog is given food from your hand.
2. Build the self control, and good focus, by gradually withdrawing your hand from protecting the ball. If the dog looses position and tries to steal the food, cover it over again with your hand. Make sure the dog remains watching the food.	If the dog holds position, watching the food when the hand is removed.	Dog is given food from your hand.

FOOD BALL STIMULATES Steps of increasing criteria | | REWARD location

3. When your hand can rest by the side of the food ball and the dog is stationary, reward by flicking the food across the floor with your index finger. The action (escaping food) will stimulate greater concentration.	Watching is increased by anticipating escaping food ball.	After the chase.
4. Teach the dog that interruption in their concentration will cause the loss of the food ball. With one hand very close to the food ball, make a noise or movement with the other hand, as the dog looks away, steal the food ball, hide it, and feign horror as the "mouse" escapes.	Lapse in concentration is punished by loss of mouse.	No reward, just set up the situation again, and reward when focus is maintained.

Add a cue prior to placing the food ball on the floor. The game can also be transferred to your hands. Flicked food drives more focus than tossed food because it is more unpredictable.

GAME 5:2 | RUN ... FAST | LEVEL 1

Developing:
HIGH DEGREE OF FOCUS
SPRINT ON CUE
DIRECTIONAL HAND
   CUES

An excellent foundation exercise for teaching a dog to go from standing still to sprint, or moving up a gear from trotting to running.

The technique of using an activity, or instinctive reaction, and preceding it with a predictable cue is easily demonstrated.

PREVIOUS SKILLS
Very good bowling skills.
Change cue technique.

RESOURCES
Sausage or cheese balls. Good surface for visible marking.

FOOD BALL STIMULATES Steps of increasing criteria	DOG is learning	REWARD location
1. Throw a food ball out for the dog to freely chase. Far enough to allow the dog to move up into a sprint. Build lots of experience, consistently throw with the same, predictable actions.	Pattern of your throwing actions. Sprinting results in reward.	Every chase is instantly rewarded, and self rewarding. No clicker needed.

If the dog is slow to chase the ball, run alongside the dog and on some occasions get there first and steal the food ball for another throw.

2. After several throws and sprint runs, as the dog turns to anticipate the next throw, turn your back on the dog and throw a food ball ahead of yourself. The dog should run past you to chase the food. Keep repeating several times.	Eating, turning and sprinting again.	At a distance, after longer sprint past you.
3. When the dog turns to look at you, insert your new cue ("run" or "fast"), turn your back to the dog and throw the food ball ahead. Take special care to get the order of this right!	Additional element of pattern - the verbal cue.	Always a reward. Fantastic game!
4. When the dog turns to look at you, give the new cue, when the dog moves into the run, click (for responding to the new cue), and turn your back to throw the food as above.	Anticipating the turn-throw-run-food sequence.	Always a reward.

VARIATIONS

RUNNING RECALL

The recall towards you at speed can be taught with slight modification. As the dog approaches you in the chase (2), turn back to face the dog and present the food ball that you held onto. After the dog has stopped in front of you, turn away from the dog again and throw the food ball to set up for another recall sprint.

Keep a good balance between maintaining the desire to run after the food ball, with the inhibited running that stops in the front of you for a recall.

RUN AND JUMP

Set up a jump behind you, and slightly to one side. Give the dog plenty of sprinting experience until the "run" behaviour is on your verbal cue.

Cue the dog to run, and then turn to throw the food through the jump. This teaches a great hand signal to jump "in this direction" and the expectation of thrown food teaches the dog to run straight after the jump.

FOLLOW THE HAND

Sprinting or even a trot can be directed with this hand signal. You can teach a dog to run towards an object (where the food will pass), or run a large circle around you (as the food is throw).

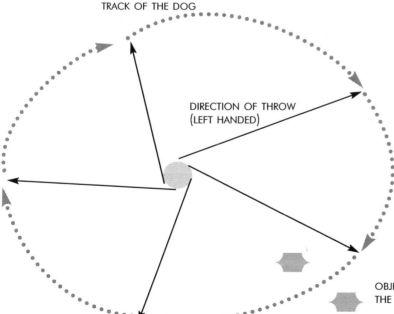

TRACK OF THE DOG

DIRECTION OF THROW
(LEFT HANDED)

OBJECTS (JUMP) CAN BE PLACED IN
THE PATH THE DOG WILL RUN

| GAME 5:3 | **WORKING AT THE DISTANCE** | LEVEL 2 |

Developing:
DISTANCE FOCUS
DISTANCE CONFIDENCE
DISTANCE BEHAVIOURS

When reviewing our teaching it becomes apparent that almost 100% of our reinforcement history (delivery of the reward) is in close proximity. The dog is quite correct in assuming, and reacting, that when they hear a click, that the place to be is near you for the food.

This can be re-balanced with plenty of training, clicks and reward at a distance.

PREVIOUS SKILLS
Good throwing skills.
Change cue technique.

RESOURCES
Sausage or cheese balls. Good surface for visible marking.

FOOD BALL STIMULATES Steps of increasing criteria	DOG is learning	REWARD location
1. With the dog at a distance, (about half way to the furthest point you can throw the food ball) teach the dog the throwing action. Either underarm as bowling; overarm - as throwing a dart; horizontal arm - as throwing a frisbee. (page 96). This must be a consistent, predictable action.	To observe and anticipate your throwing pattern.	Behind and beyond the dog. Easily seen for chasing and collection.
2. Only commence the throwing action, (moving the arm to throw), when the dog looks at you. If they are still hunting the floor with their eyes, do not move. You can click the visual check-in if you think it will help the dog.	To check in, which triggers the next throw sequence.	Behind and beyond the dog.
3. As the dog looks at you, begin the opening arm movement by taking the hand back for the swing. Stop the movement at this point. When the dog has stood still, continue and let the food ball release. You can use a clicker as well if it makes it clearer for the dog.	When the arm begins the movement, food ball will come, so STAND STILL and wait for food.	Behind and beyond the dog.
4. Using the new cue / old cue technique, add a verbal cue ("out" or "stop") before any move of the throwing arm. Continue repeating the same action sequence as in 3. Look for the dog anticipating the standing still, click anticipation and follow through with the throw.	To anticipate on the new cue.	Behind and beyond the dog.
5. Once the dog is predictably stopping at the distance and holds the position as soon as they have eaten the reward, begin to insert on-cue behaviours before the click. Verbally cued behaviours are most effective at the distance, rather than hand signals.	Focus, observe, listen for cued behaviour, and hold position after click.	Behind and beyond the dog, or direct to the dog's mouth if you are exceptionally good at throwing!

VARIATIONS

FREE SHAPING AT THE DISTANCE

This is especially beneficial to build confidence at the distance. Moves that have been shaped close to you can be duplicated through the same path at the distance.

Begin with shaping the dog to return to a large rug or sheet spread on the floor at the distance, but not further than your effective throws, after each reward is eaten. This is your "shaping home spot". once the dog is reliably returning, begin to shape established behaviours at this distance, looking for the same learning pathway. Shaping to targets may be a useful prompt.

STOP POSITIONS OF THE RECALL

The "stop" technique can be used in combination with the "Run .. Fast" (Game 5:2 page 101) to teach the positions on a running recall. The outcome is a fast start to the recall, quickly into a position, then fast recall to you.

The dog begins from the stationary position, (sit or down), is called towards you on "fast" cue, and several times the predicted food going past the handler.

Intermittently, the handler turns back to face the dog for the "stop" stationary cue and gives a position cue, this can be rewarded with the "fast" cue, the handler turns away and throws the food etc.

It is essential that the dog has plenty of practise of "stop" and "run .. fast" gmes separately before combining the two. Then a mixed, unpredictable pattern of both games to ensure a fresh reaction to each cue. Both behaviours are contradictory to each other and must be carefully balanced.

ADD THE CUE

The cue "out", or "stop" can be added, and should be regarded as a separate behaviour that is rewarded in its own right, rather than the subsequent behaviours.

Avoid using the cues for established behaviours to stop the dog, such as sit or down. If these were taught in close proximity the dog will try to return to that spot for the reinforcement.

The routine will be: run towards you, "stop", click, throw reward; "stop, sit", click, throw reward etc.

GAME 5:4

THIS WAY

LEVEL 1

Developing:
TURN IN FULL SPRINT
RUN THIS WAY

This behaviour can be a lifesaving behaviour. When taught carefully, practised regularly and rigorously it can be used to stop a dog in full flight after a rabbit.

Using the dog's innate desire to co-operatively hunt, a verbal cue or whistle, will be used to turn the dog away from what they are chasing to join you in the chase for your object / prey (ie; the ball or food ball).

PREVIOUS SKILLS
Run Fast Game (5:2).
Good throwing skills.
Change cue technique.

RESOURCES
Very large sausage or cheese balls. Outdoor, fenced area. Short grass.

FOOD BALL STIMULATES Steps of increasing criteria	DOG is learning	REWARD location
1. Refresh the Run ... Fast Game (5:2). Change the "run" or "fast" cue to the dog's name, a whistle, or the cue "this way". As the dog begins to run towards you, reward this with the throw, and additionally you run to the thrown food or ball as well. This will stimulate your dog to maintain speed and get to the prize first. To keep this competitive, make sure to give yourself one or two handicapped throws where you can succeed in reaching the prize first.	On the new cue, to sprint, VERY fast past you or possibly lose the prize.	Ahead of both you and the dog.
2. Once this behaviour is well established, set the dog up to chase one food ball and when half way to that food ball, give your "turn away" cue and proceed as above. The added stimulus of you sprinting after a different reward should turn the dog away from the food they are chasing. If there is no turn response, give the cue to turn away almost as soon as you have thrown the first food/ball. Try to make the second prize closer to achieve. The closer the dog is to the first prize, the harder it is to turn the dog away.	To turn off one prize for the opportunity for a possibly better prize.	When the dog successfully turns when in full sprint, reward with the second prize, plus several short throw and chases, making this the super prize.

Keep the behaviour fresh and practise separately. If the dog experiences too many calls to turn away from chasing a prize, they will begin to slow down or stop. This may be useful if you never want the dog to chase, but it will also inhibit the variations of Games in 5:2.

6 GAMES From the Dog

Dogs dance naturally. It is often their expression of happiness and different situations which cause them to "dance". My Gordon pup destined for search rescue used to accompany me up the hill to count sheep at post lambing time when they needed a nightly check over. He was not interested in sheep but loved to pick up the air rising up the hill and pirouetted to catch the various flavours. I think the wind on the hill top skipped this way and that and brought all the rich smells of the valley up to pass his nose. He "danced" in the wind.

Today, two collie siblings play together in the garden. They both have a toy which they consider better than anything else on offer. To tempt their play partner they dance around, toss the toy in the air, shake it, leave it on the ground and dance around it, pouncing and twisting every which way.

We have the ability to capture these moments and the sense of well being they bring. Only a dog in full health, secure and content would display these behaviours. Play is nature's way of exploring learning, and only occurs when the animal is well.

It is a point of discussion as to whether actions that are stimulated by an emotion, can be captured to re-stimulate the emotion. Can we trigger the happy feelings? Can we change emotions by changing the behaviour, and can we change behaviours by changing the emotions? We have evidence for the latter, and I am searching for evidence for the former.

Free shaping dance movements vary from whole body patterns to small movements of just the face and feet.

ONLY YOUR ....

One of the great shaping, and learning, skills is to communicate that it is a specialised part of the movement or action that we want to capture. A paw movement is easy to stimulate, but we must always consider what the rest of the dog's body is doing. If captured in the sit, then inevitably when a "paw" is cued the dog will adopt the sit.

When capturing small actions, if we successfully isolate them on cue then a great variety of combination movements can be designed.

This is excellent learning practice for the dog. It teaches them a tight focus on one small action, whilst the rest of their body supports the movements. Small on cue actions teach flexibility and new movements. Rarely would a dog sit in the beg position and wash its face - this is not quite a natural behaviour. But by teaching the "beg", "both paws", and "face" we can engineer a composite, new behaviour.

Where possible the small actions will be captured after the rest of the body has been placed into a stationary hold. We can shape movements of the head once the dog is in a settled, lying down position. By holding the rest of the body "off duty" the dog can focus on a smaller movement, rather than a gross movement.

To achieve this the foundation behaviour for much of the small action shaping is to lock the dog into the background position. For example, cue the experienced dog, or shape a new dog, into the settled down position, and make sure the food is delivered so that the dog does not have to move after a click. This is not necessarily into the dog's mouth, but food can easily be placed in "The Pocket", the area under the dog's head and between the front legs. After 10 or 15 repetitions a withheld click should not result in the dog getting up, but staying in position and perhaps initiating a small movement of their head or front legs.

Arnold learned an entire chain of nine behaviours from this start point:

"Are you ready?"   in the play bow

"You really need to sit"   hips would drop into the lion down position

"Are you comfortable?"   rock into in the settled hip position

"You look a bit untidy"   tuck a front paw under

"Would you like to go shopping"? drop head into sleepy position

" .. or rather play cricket?"   head would shoot up, alert and interested

"We could always play football"   roll onto side in the flat down position

"What do you think of ******?"   raise one back leg to vertical position

(*** is usually substituted for the location of the demonstration)

"no, no, what do you REALLY think of....?" roll onto back with feet over face

At this point the reinforcement from the laughing audience would finish the chain.

He learned these behaviours all from the down position, he offered what he thought was good at the time, and we built the chain. I selected what he offered to allow a step by step progression, but these were all natural behaviours for him. He often used to sleep with one leg in the air or on his back. It was an excellent exercise in self awareness, creativity, and developed excellent memory skills.

WALTZ, SALSA OR NUTCRACKER SUITE?

Besides learning how to select and control one small part of their bodies. Dogs are excellent at learning movement patterns, especially if these patterns are naturally chosen.

When training Tessie to put her front feet on a mat, she was so obsessive about the food that she never looked for the mat, but would jigger around on the spot waiting for it to arrive under her feet. This began to show a regular pattern, and when I removed the mat we were left with a great jazz dance step: back two steps, side two steps, forward forward stand still.

The key with teaching repetitive patterns is to begin the dog from exactly the same point every time. Something about that situation or placement relative to you triggers the movements. You can extend the movements or let them repeat and build a small dance routine.

GAME 6:1 — Free movement: MARCHING — LEVEL 2

Developing:
SMALL ACTIONS
LEFT FROM RIGHT
CONTROLLED BALANCE

The most naturally shaped paw action is the on the spot stepping.
Individual paw actions are best captured through targets for each paw.

You will need exceptionally good observation skills to be able to anticipate the movements, and to replace the dog in the opening position with the lure reward.

PREVIOUS SKILLS
Free shaping.

RESOURCES
None.

PATTERN OF PROGRESS Steps of increasing criteria	CLICK to mark	REWARD location
1. Begin with the dog in a standing position in front of you. Look for slight changes in balance*.	Shifting balance.	Opening position.
2. Increase the degree of shifting until the dog seems to be swaying from side to side.	Increased shift in balance, both ways.	Opening position.
3. Look for a lift of one paw or the other, or a step forwards or sideways.	Paws moving.	Opening position.
4. Increase the degree of movement and repetition.	Paws moving higher or faster.	Opening position.

You can evolve a deliberate swaying movement with the paw lift, or a fast jigging on the spot with the dog tapping on the floor, allow the movement to develop as the dog suggests.

5. The movement of the back paws can be taught in the same way, although it is harder to capture.	Back paw movement.	Opening position.

* Remember that your body language will have a strong effect on the dog.
If you sit peering at the dog like it is tomorrow's dinner, he will feel very uncomfortable, and unlikely to offer free spirited movement.
If you sit frozen still, the dog is likely to copy you.
Try to incorporate a relaxed watching, with interest but not fixation. Be animated in your delivery of rewards, and maybe even play with the rewards in your hands, fidget in your chair to open up the conversation of movement.

GAME 6:2 | Free movement: HEAD | LEVEL 1

Developing:

SELF INITIATED ACTION

LEFT FROM RIGHT

OFF FOCUS

PREVIOUS SKILLS

None, ideal beginners.

Advanced movements need shaping experience.

This is a fundamental learning exercise that is perfect for teaching self awareness of small actions. Ideal for first learners.

4   learning to control head movement in a specific direction and specific angle

4   teaches the dog to take their focus away from the food

It would be tempting to use targets for this movement, but the dog is very likely to focus on the interaction with the target, rather than the movement that results in the interaction.

For this learning it is beneficial to be a free shaped movement, WITHOUT target or luring. It is the most likely action to teach the concept of a self initiated action.

RESOURCES

None.

PATTERN OF PROGRESS Steps of increasing criteria

PATTERN OF PROGRESS Steps of increasing criteria	CLICK to mark	REWARD location
1. Begin with the dog comfortably maintaining a fixed position such as the sit or down.	Maintain relaxed position.	Feed in position.
2. For first learners, accept any movement of the head. This maybe sideways in response to an external noise, or a dip to sniff the floor etc.	Any head movement.	Take the head back to the neutral opening position.
3. Establish familiarity with the small movement before increasing the action. Let the dog develop their sense of awareness.	Look for the "aha" building with the movement.	Take the head back to the neutral opening position.
4. Build the degree of the movement and increase fluency. Speed of movement will naturally build the size of the movement as the momentum increases.	The larger movements.	Turn the head in the opposing direction to feed.

VARIATIONS

Teach head turns to both directions to ensure balanced muscle development. Make sure the chin stays level and the dog's eye contact with you and the food is broken. Maintaining eye contact will inhibit the movement.

TURNING IN A CIRCLE

It is not difficult to progress this opening movement into a full circle. As soon as the head momentum increases begin to mark the movement of the front feet to support the movement, until the dog is stepping away.

Increase the criteria to a full circle. Once the behaviour gets momentum the dog can quickly distort the movement into a flip. Not suitable for freestyle training where a target stick nose will secure a better shaped circle.

Teach both directions to ensure balanced flexibility.

HEAD NODS AND SLEEPY HEADS

A Head Nod is a different muscle movement to a sleepy head.

The nod brings the chin down onto the chest.

The Sleepy Head, stretches the neck forwards for a chin on the floor when in the down position, or resting on an object or hand.

Avoid confusing the two actions. Both are excellent exercise and learning strategies for a dog with restricted mobility.

HEAD COCKED IN QUERY?

The only success I have had in capturing this is by stimulating the movement with a whinning or pitiful noise.

Use the original stimulus to build and perfect the movement and then transfer to a new cue.

ADD THE CUES

Each action deserves its own cue. Head movements towards an object or person can become great tricks with hand signals.

When speaking about a particular topic: "would you like to go shopping?" you can give the hand signal for Sleepy, and "would you like to play football?" give the signal for alert leap up or head cock.

Similarly, "who is the best player?" and you hold your hand behind the person you want the dog to look at.

GAME 6:3

Free movement: FACE

LEVEL 1

Developing:
TINY ACTIONS
CHANGING EMOTION
WOW! ITS ME?

PREVIOUS SKILLS
None.
Perfect for learning inhibited dogs.

Learning to move only tiny parts of the facial muscles is a very high degree of self awareness and control. People have a problem raising just one eyebrow, let alone moving individual ears.

Dogs can use all these muscles with finesse to change facial expressions. For dogs that are in a slightly anxious situation, captured movement of the face will increase relaxation and you will see the dog become more comfortable.

4   learning to control very fine movements

4   learning to separate body language

RESOURCES
None.

PATTERN OF PROGRESS Steps of increasing criteria	CLICK to mark	REWARD location
1. Begin with the dog comfortably maintaining a fixed position such as the sit or down.	Maintain relaxed position.	Feed to maintain position.
2. For new learners select a facial movement that the dog initiates, and build as desired.	Click for movement.	Feed to maintain position.

Make sure the movement stays isolated from other actions, keep a relaxed pace to the food delivery.

VARIATIONS

Most of the facial movements can be stimulated.

The stimulus is the cue and to be able to gain fluency through repetition select stimulus under your control.

You may get a wonderful facial expressions as your dog passes wind, but this is one stimulus outside the realms of our control. Fluency would be unhealthy to achieve!

LICKING LIPS

Hmmm .... tasty. This licking should not be a signal of anxiety.

Stimulate with tasty treats, particularly the variety that spreads around the mouth, and residue could be wiped around the lips. Squeezy cheese, patè, crumbled liver, honey on a spoon.

NOSE WRINKLES OR SMILES

Some dogs perform this behaviour when greeting as an appeasement behaviour. Ideal to capture when offered.

You may be able to stimulate the behaviour when offering food very slowly, where the dog begins to pull back their lips to take the food.

Not suitable for all dogs.

EAR FLICKS

If the dog is intently focussed on the training, your food and possible signals, a distant noise will trigger acknowledgement with a movement of the ear but not sufficient interest for a full head turn.

Test out a few noises that you can manage or are predictable.

Tone of voice or your animated conversation can elicit ear movement.

ADD THE CUE

Most of these behaviours will be stimulated by another event.

Manage these stimulus, build the quality and fluency, and then transfer to final cue.

GAME 6:4

Free movement: RELAX

Developing:

RELAXING THE MUSCLES

RELAXED DURATION

ASSOCIATION OF
SECURITY

PREVIOUS SKILLS

Using an alternative
marker.

Hand contact for reward.

Clicker training is rather counter productive to teaching relaxed behaviours.
The click triggers a sense of excitement and success, a "wow" moment,
getting it right and the promise of something they like. Training with a click
encourages activity, managed excitement, anticipation and interaction.

Relaxation needs the opposite: a sense of security, comfort, slowing heart
beat and anticipation of sleep.

As the learning progresses the behaviour can be marked either with a
verbal marker, or hand contact.

The reward will be a long, gentle stroking that stimulates more relaxation

RESOURCES

Warm, comfortable and secure environment.

PATTERN OF PROGRESS Steps of increasing criteria	TOUCH to mark	STROKE location
1. Make sure the environment will induce a sense of security, comfort for both you and the dog. Begin with the dog within hand range and stroke for 3 seconds. When the dog moves closer or requests more attention, begin the stroking again.	A pro-active desire to continue.	Dog's flank or sternum.

Try to induce the leg joints to relax. The outcome of completely relaxed joints will
eventually be a roll onto a flat position. Gradually progress the dog to this point.

2. Check the face is relaxed, with good even breathing, and no evident stress to the tongue, which should be floppy, soft ears and eyes. Where you stroke will induce relaxation. For floppy eared dogs, take up the weight of the ears in your hand and massage the base of the ear.	A pro-active desire to continue. Every time the dog seeks more contact, keeping the action very slow.	Under the chin, finger tips on top of head, down ears.
3. Massage around the shoulder joints and then the hips joints. As soon as the dog shows progress in its relaxtion, move onto stroking that area.	The action of relaxing, continues the stoking.	Flat palm of hand slowly from skull to base of tail.
4. Stroking of the flank, the inner thigh and under the chest will encourage the dog to promote that area for more exposure. These are good signs of relaxation.	Complete relaxtion, trust in your hands, keeps the stroking.	Lots of flat palm contact on trunk of body.

A cue for this relaxation process can be added from the hand contact. The area you
massage and stroke is the point you want the dog to relax.

7 GAMES
Self Control

Self Control is one of the greatest gifts you can give a youngster. Learning self control is the process of growing up. It means we can't have what we want when we want it. We may need to save our money, save up holiday time or wait until we have a bigger property before we have another puppy. I don't remember it being an easy learning curve, it was mostly painful disappointment, and I spent much of my energy trying to work around the barriers!

Self control encompasses the ability to ignore distractions, to be able to concentrate on the job in hand. To learn to not chase something just because it is moving. To learn to get excited but not go over the top. We love our puppies for various reasons, but often we inadvertently love their lack of self control. Their spontaneous reaction to a leaf blowing, their joy at seeing our face again, their pleasure in spending time with us, watching them play with a toy. Without paying attention we reinforce these behaviours. Growing up is not the total end to all fun, just a change in the fun. We start to play more adult games where the thin line of success is only a step away from losing.

We all need to teach our dogs self control. This is the centre of living in our society. Learning to not bark at all the neighbours activities, keep a focus on you when out in the park, not get over excited with visitors, not chase other dogs, cats, children, bikes, cars etc etc. By teaching self control with games we manage to keep the fun in the learning and have exceptionally good response to the control tools in the process.

There are many people who make a living from what we would consider games: tennis, golf, card games, surfing; activities can be fun or seriously competitive. The same will be for your dogs, some will regard the games as pure fun and enjoyment (just to please you) others will be deadly serious in their desire to win.

GAMES NEED RULES

Without rules, games with the dogs can go wrong very quickly. We may be playing tug games with the dog, but "accidentally" the dog/pup bites our hand holding the toy. If this became a habit, not only would we never want to play again, but we would also teach the dog that when a hand is holding a toy, the toy becomes the dogs, should they bite the hand. REALLY bad learning, with no future.

If two dogs are playing tug it frequently ends with one winning possession. The tactic is to begin to move your own mouth nearer to the opposition until they back down and drop their end. It is not an accident, progression up the toy is a challenge. You will resolve it with an instant end of the game and the habit nipped in the bud as soon as possible. This is a rule, and you will need to stick to it if you want to play tug games with your dog in future.

SELF CONTROL IS A MUSCLE

If you view self control as a muscle, then you can build the appropriate strength with regular repetition, increasing opposition (weights), and increased duration. You will build flexibility with a range of games and transfers the learning to real life situations.

The young Boxer Boy that can maintain a self imposed sit whilst the toy flies around the room is going to be able to transfer that self control to greeting children. We will make several transition stages to explain the process, but just as a target object can trigger a behaviour a toy can also be a target that cues self control. The toy passes to the child and the dog will manage self control for the child.

HUNT CHASE KILL RIP

Most games you play with the dog that have high levels of excitement come from the hunt chain. These are intrinsically dangerous for the prey, and can also be harmful to the predator and the peer hunters.

Safety for you, the dog and the environment is a first priority. New toys can always be purchased, but your back is not replaceable. A bad jump for a toy can twist a leg, and injury will mean no games for several weeks.

REWARDS

Rewards during games will vary from dog to dog. Learn to observe how your dog likes to play with other dogs. See what they enjoy the most. Some prefer to chase, some prefer to tug. You will only be able to assess what is rewarding by the fact that the behaviour you have just rewarded gets stronger. Play can be rewarded at several levels, by increasing the intensity at a high level, or just remaining frozen still at a low level.

THE CLICKER

For most of the games you will need a clicker. If your dog has only paired a click and food, take some time pairing the toy game with the click. Begin to play and quietly click as you enjoy the process, build up the level or arousal, make it more exciting and click frequently as you play.

The games will change in reward intensity, you may want to click the dog for making eye contact whilst holding the toy. The click can be followed by a more exciting tug session.

When using a clicker in play be very, very stringent about the the timing of your cue "play". If you allow the dog to begin the game on the click this would be the same as allowing the dog to snatch the food from your hand or reward reserve. You control the access to the food, equally you must control the access to the game.

The routine will be:

> CLICK (count 3 seconds)   .... CUE "PLAY" ...... PRESENT THE TOY

When building instinctive reactions the successful behaviour is followed almost simultaneously with the continuation of the game. Even I can't always get a click in these moments. So when the reward is as close as it can be to the behaviour you are trying to build, such as a good solid grip, you do not need to try and use the clicker. Leave it for the moments where there is a gap between the learning and the reward.

PUNISHMENT

Inevitably mistakes will be made and the dog will explore a tactic that has no future. Mostly these errors are a result of over enthusiasm, or lack of control in the aroused state.

The errors could be: biting your hand
                      pushing against you with their feet
                      jumping up to snatch the toy in your hands

All will result in punishment, which in our world is a loss of play opportunity.

AWWWW ... NO MORE FUN ROUTINE:
   1. Take the toy, bunch it tightly in your hands and hold against your chest.

The dog must not be allowed access to the toy at all. If the dog continues to lunge at you for the toy, use a book (not this one!) or clip board to divert the lunge.

2. Stand facing a wall or barrier, that prevents the dog finding access to the front of you.

3. Avoid eye contact and stay in that position for 15 seconds, perhaps more.

As soon as the time is complete turn around and carry on playing as if nothing happened (even though your fingers are still throbbing). If the same error happens again lengthen the time to 30 seconds. Usually errors repeat because the dog is getting tired, loosing concentration or they have gone too far over the top, they are over aroused. A longer time down period, to reduce arousal, gives more chance for recovery. If there is a third repetition of the same error, then the dog is too tired, or too aroused for the situation. Put the toy away, take a complete break for the day.

AROUSAL

The dog will become more aroused in the game, ie: more excited and less able to control themselves because:

1. The game has become closer to the critical kill.

2. The game has gone on for a long time.

When both elements are together the level of arousal can shoot through the roof and the dog will have no chance to regain self control.

The measure of arousal is the ability of the dog to respond to self control, cooling down, and responding to the cue for a known behaviour. If you take the toy from the dog but they immediately jump at you to recapture it, they are over aroused. You can use a less exciting toy, play for a shorter time, or play a less exciting game. Throughout play time you must teach yourself to be constantly aware of the building arousal and onset of tiredness.

As you build the dog's skill to change from arousal to control, you will increase the toy value, the game value or the duration, but only one element at a time. Being able to play for longer will develop mental stamina and longer duration of concentration skills.

COOL DOWN

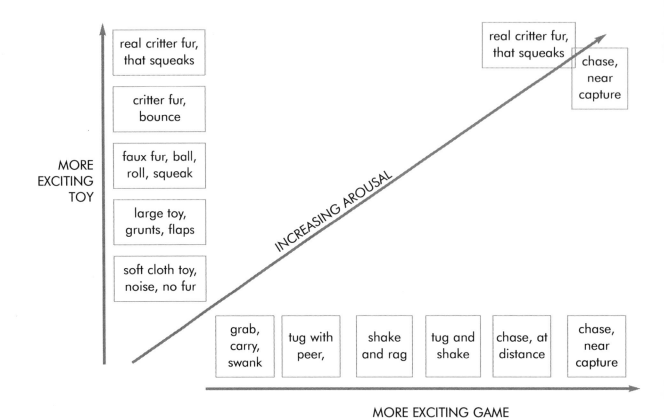

MORE EXCITING GAME

Each dog will have their own variations on the level of toys that cause arousal and types of games that cause excitement. Experience and practice will also change their perceptions.

Nearly all dogs will become quickly aroused playing with real fur, on a toy that squeaks at the point they are just about to kill. Once your mouth surrounds the prey, and the prey is still alive and escapes, that recapture will be the fastest and strongest bite in the dog's history.

When building arousal take time to also teach a cool down. When you take the toy, nine out of 10 times the dog will go back into play, on the tenth occasion Game time will end. Develop a routine to end the play: take the toy, tuck it out of sight (I usually flick it under my armpit), show the dog empty hands, put the dog back on lead, or settle them down and leave them for at least 10 minutes. I use this time to write notes.

You can then begin the Games again in cycle of Games, cool down, games, cool down etc. The length of game time will depend on the dog's physical fitness, mental stamina, and self control strength.

WHY PLAY GAMES?

Games, or play time, is nature's school room. Young lambs, with full tummies and the sun on their backs will play at flocking, running races close together, being king of the castle; puppies will wrestle, stalk, rip toys, carry and explore. All of these behaviours are rehearsals for real life. This is where the life skills are learned. Collies practice stalking each other, the Gordon's point at Blue Tits, they all practice one-up-man-ship with possession of valued objects, eating, initiating play etc.

During a game the mind is often focussed on success in the game, which drives the player to try harder not to lose. Small losses are learning experiences, the natural to and fro between two players, but both players will avoid a white wash.

During the games our senses are at their very finest. Physically everything is running on full power, we are mentally alert, ultra observant, totally focussed and go beyond our natural caution. This is the dog I want as my partner, particularly in work, competition or performance situations.

Clicker training has expanded our ability to teach nearly every dog a good range of behaviours. We have a call in from the garden, a sit when guests arrive, a wait whilst the car is opened. And we all know these are perfect when there is nothing else more rewarding or exciting on offer. By playing games and bringing these behaviours into the game, we teach the dog, that in the exciting situation of the game, the game will only continue when these behaviours occur.

The continuation gives a strong reward for correct repose and the dog learns to carry out the behaviour in more arousing situations. This is the true function of "play" = rehearsal for real life.

During hunt games with pack members a deepening of the pack bond occurs. Dogs hunt co-operatively and often kill as a group, particularly large prey that requires several dogs to dispatch. Not only will you build exceptional conditioning through association that you are an essential member of the team, but co-operation is the access to more exciting and thrilling chases, capture and destroy opportunities.

You will also learn the hidden depths of your dog's personality that may not surface in other situations. Their determination or sensitivity. Their commitment or easy going acceptance of loss. You will see their focus develop, their raw nature emerge. Sometime this is quite alarming, but quite normal, and you may see responses that surprise you.

AWAKENING FRIGHTENING INSTINCTS

A dog that is highly aroused may bite you. As you take the toy, if it moves with any degree of animation the dog's instinct will be to grab it again. Make a habit of keeping your arms very still, the toy quite limp and only move it into your containment (It's Mine) position very carefully and without sudden movement. If the toy flips up into the air and you jiggle it fast to catch hold the dog may perceive the toy (prey) as still alive and on the point of escaping again. Their instinctive reaction, a without thought reaction, will be to get their teeth around the toy and assist you in the final kill.

If your dog is low on instinctive reactions this is a key moment to try to arouse them. The prey would not jump back into their mouth, but make every attempt to escape. If on the end of a Whippit, it is easy to simulate a dying gasp from the prey and arouse the dog's instinct for the final kill. But avoid pushing the toy back at the dog, get dramatic about the pending escape and join your partner in the re-capture.

If the dog releases the toy frequently, or the mouth chomps up and down, take the toy away at ANY opportunity and launch into a co-operative chase.

As you play, remember you are simulating the kill instinct in your dog. You will control this through the game, and be left with a highly focussed, competitive, partner.

TOYS

Look for toys that are comfortable for both you and the dog. Sadly most pet shops suppliers are not dog play partners and often the products for sale are not suitable for our types of games.

Avoid:

HARD ROPE BALLS/TUGS: these can cut the gums, and without any elasticity they will jar your shoulder and probably the dog's neck.

TENNIS BALLS: only use these in moderation, the material can disintegrate easily on the cheaper products, mostly the ones supplied as pet toys, the surface material can wear down teeth enamel.

Look for:

TUGS: plaited fabric with some degree of give. Fleece or soft cloth that can be washed. A knot for more secure dog grip, and a handle for your hand. Long enough for play without bending over.

FOOD BAG: a fabric bag or sock containing food, that can be tied to the Whippit or onto a tug handle.

REAL OR FAUX FUR: that can be wrapped around or integrated into something more robust, such as the tug toy

HANDLING SKILLS

Holding the clicker and the toy is a challenge by itself. Practice before you start a game, and don't be surprised if there are a few more wild clicks in this sport. You will need to access the clicker with speed. The nature of the games mean that behaviours you are looking for happen very fast.

Learn to use the Whippit:

Practice moving the toy around you at ground level.

Lighter toys are easier to keep mobile and animated.

Flick the toy from a 12 o'clock position to a 6 o'clock position rapidly.

Set a target on the ground and practice landing the toy on the target.

Drop the toy on target and twirl the handle enough to make the toy appear to be in its last dying gasps.

Work out a strategy where you can comfortably manoeuvre the toy on the Whippit and use the clicker.

GAME 7:1 | Self Control: CHIPS OR ME? | LEVEL 1

Developing:
REWARD RULES
SELF CONTROL

This is the fundamental learning exercise for all food or reward training. The stronger the desire for the reward, the stronger the behaviour will become. Dogs with very high interest in the reward food can become a nuisance and fixate on the food, mug your hands or be unable to concentrate on the learning. The food becomes a distraction rather than simple motivation.

The presence, or scent, of food should stimulate the default behaviour of "What can I do for you?" in the dog. Establish this with different types of food and later different toys.

PREVIOUS SKILLS

Holding the food reserve and clicker in the same hand.

Nose to hand target or nose to target stick.

RESOURCES
Target stick, hand or object

PATTERN OF PROGRESS Steps of increasing criteria　　　CLICK to mark　　　REWARD location

1. Sit at eye level to the dog and place several pieces of food in one hand at nose height. Make sure the dog is aware of the food. Lightly cage your hand so that self rewarding is not possible. Allow the dog to pester your hand.	Any pause, step back caused by frustration.	With your other hand take a piece of the food and give to direct to the dog.

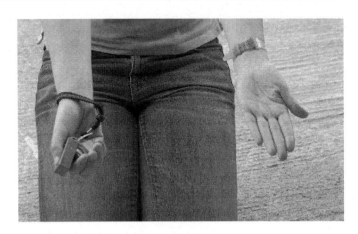

2. Encourage the dog to acknowledge the presence of food and reward the dog for remembering that moving away from the food gets the food.	Obvious step back, or gesture of self control.	With your other hand take a piece of the food and give direct to the dog.

3. Refresh the target behaviour: either nose to target hand, or nose to target stick. Sit with both the caged food and the target hand offered equidistant from the dog's nose. They should be able to touch either by a simple movement of their head. The choice is "Chips or Me?".	Touching the target: moving away from the food to perform a simple, correct behaviour with focus.	With your target hand take a piece of the food and give direct to the dog.

Pay great attention to the quality of the target behaviour. It should be perfect, no half measures or excuses for anything less than the best performance.

4. Begin to extend the distance to the target, even placing the target behind the dog so that they need to remember the target themselves, not be prompted by the visual cue.	Touching the target.	Piece of the food delivered by target hand.
5. Build for duration of a stationary behaviour or develop a self check in to you in the presence of a food container on the floor or at nose level, with the dog on lead.	Duration, focus away from food for longer period.	Food delivered by hand direct to the dog.

WALKING ON LEAD CONTROL

1. Place a piece of food at nose level (on a chair or stool), and place your lightly caged hand over the food. Reward for Step 1 and 2 in this situation. Extend the control to placing the food on the floor.	Obvious step back, or gesture of self control.	With your other hand pick up the piece of the food and give to the dog.
2. Place the food on a specific marker such as a mat or the food pot lid. Establish self control with the dog remaining stationary at your side, on lead, at 10 paces.	Self initiated check in to you.	Take one step towards food pot.
3. Gradually close the distance to the food marker (reward station) one pace at a time. On successful check in take a step closer, if loss of control take one step back away from food.	Increasing self control as you get closer to reward station becomes harder.	Take step towards food pot. On arrival YOU pick up food to give direct to dog.

GREETING CONTROL

1. With the same process as above, place the person or the dog that causes the loss of self control behind the reward station. Go through the same step by step approach, always control the reward yourself, do not allow self rewarding access.	

ADD THE CUE

The reward itself becomes the cue for self control. Do not add a verbal "control" cue. This is the permanent life long cue of a world filled with opportunities for reward: Access in and out of the door, in and out of the car, on and off lead, greeting you, getting a fuss from you, intermittent treats, dinner, grooming.

The dog will develop a good, well mannered attitude that rewards are plentiful when asked for with courtesy and not demanded as their right.

GAME 7:2

Self Control: GIVE AND TAKE

Developing:
  SELF CONTROL
  GOOD MANNERS
  CONTROLLED TAKE

PREVIOUS SKILLS
Toy hold with a good grip.

To be able to teach a Give we need a confident hold. Most puppies will grab moving articles, but if your dog is over sensitive, play the "Building Arousal" games to acquire a confident hold before practising Give exercises.

This is a key learning exercise that becomes the basis for teaching control of arousal and gives excellent stimulus control training opportunities.

When offering the toy to the dog, make sure you can replicate the gesture and verbal cue with a safe presentation of the toy, with the part you want the dog to grip nearest and most attractive.

RESOURCES
Attractive tough, toy. Strong back and arms.

PATTERN OF PROGRESS Steps of increasing criteria

	CLICK to mark	REWARD game
1. Begin with the dog under control, focussed on you. This can be any position, location in front of you. Hold the toy at waist height, after the click, cue "play" and offer the toy.	Evidence of self control, no anticipation.	Play for short time until good grip.
2. When the dog has a good grip pull the dog towards you on the toy. The hand without the clicker goes under the dog's neck to get hold of the collar, with your palm uppermost. Hold onto the collar just to prevent continuation of any pull action. Keep perfectly still.	For the collar hold and stillness.	Release collar and restart play for short time (3 seconds).
3. Repeat the collar hold and keep a slight upward tension on the toy. Relax and prevent game continuation. The dog's jaw should relax slightly, or even let go of the toy.	Jaw slackening or release of toy.	Release collar and restart play for short time (3 seconds).
4. Only reward the increasing relaxation of the toy, until there is a full release. For determined dogs or highly aroused dogs, this may take several minutes.	Jaw slackening or release of toy.	Release collar and restart play for short time (3 seconds).
5. Make sure on release the dog can move their head away from the toy, release the collar grip as soon as the dog releases the toy. Look for the dog "giving up" the toy to you, not just being able to take it from the dog. A polite attitude is very important, it is YOUR toy.	Release of toy AND courtesy backward move.	Restart play for short time (3 seconds).

ADD THE CUE

This is a critical cue and a foundation for self control in the future.

Before your hand moves to hold the collar, stand quite still, not participating but still holding the toy with the dog, and give the verbal "off" or "give" cue. Then follow the usual collar hold, wait, dog release's toy sequence.

As soon as the dog anticipates the sequence and gives up the toy on the verbal cue. Take the whole toy very slowly into your hands and hold it close to your chest. This is a dangerous moment, you are no longer holding the collar and the dog is very likely to jump up to catch the toy.

As soon as you have achieved containment, click and restart the play.

DEVELOPMENT

The verbal "off" cue can also be equated to "end all kill process", which can be very successfully transferred to a real life chase.

Once the dog is skilled at the release sequence increase the criteria and cue the release during play, not just when you are both still and partly under control. Begin with only a low level of arousal.

Develop the skill through to the point where your release cue will stop the dog before they take hold of the toy. Begin with a stationary toy, and then move onto the toy on the Whippit. You must be in a position to remove the toy if the dog does not respond to the cue.

KEEP IT HEALTHY

Always practice a high proportion of release behaviours to end of game behaviour. If every release ends the game completely you will begin to sour the release behaviour and trigger a reluctance.

For dogs that like the chase and herd part of the game more than the capture, the release sequence is followed by their most rewarding part of the game, and can become too easily self initiating by the dog.

Only respond to the release when you have the behaviour you desire: a placement to your hand, or drop on the floor by your feet. Avoid rewarding the dog for dropping the toy further and further out of reach.

GAME 7:3

Tactics: BUILD AROUSAL

LEVEL 2

Developing:
INSTINCTIVE
    REACTIONS
PREY STALK
GRIP POWER
PLAY CONFIDENCE

Some dogs are over sensitive to playing these sort of games with you, their Higher Being. Tug games are mostly played between siblings and peers, and used to explore the hierarchy within the relationship. If your dog considers themselves extremely low status, they will need to have their confidence developed to be able to enjoy the games.

PREVIOUS SKILLS
Whippit handling

RESOURCES
Whippit, faux fur, squeaker, bouncer.

DEVELOPING AROUSAL STRATEGIES

A. Using the Whippit, make sure the toy is as far away from you as possible on the end of the line. Your proximity can be over whelming. Every time the dog captures the toy, give small shakes to stimulate life in the critter.

B. Keep your body language non-confrontational. Do not face the dog frontally. Turn your head away, play pathetically weak, and allow the dog to pull you along.

C. When the dog self releases the toy, make sure it escapes very fast, but encourage re-capture. The arousal level is at its highest in the situation of going hungry again.

D. Build up the amount of chase before capture. The extra effort will arouse the dog physically building a strong bite when the opportunity is given.
    Let the dog chase in very close proximity, with lots of air snaps and frustrating near misses.

E. If the dog is keen on the toy but not strong on chasing. Reward the chasing actions with the click and flick the toy towards the dog. Any brave attempts to chase are rewarded by the (stupid) prey coming towards the dog for a capture.

GAME 7:4 — Self Control: GRIP & CARRY — LEVEL 1

Developing:

CONTINUAL GRIP

CLEAN PICK UP

CLEAN CARRY AND APPROACH

Many breeds do not have an instinctive strong bite. Their background skills may have been developed for other instincts, such as herding, scent quartering, companion etc.

This game will not make their jaw stronger, but make sure that a slack mouth, or re-gripping mouth is not rewarded. For dogs without strong jaw muscles, temper your pull and only nudge or coax the toy. Some dogs cannot physically grip tight.

PREVIOUS SKILLS

Whippit handling

RESOURCES

Easily gripped toy on Whippit. A large toy that fills the mouth displacing the grip per tooth power to all the teeth.

PATTERN OF PROGRESS Steps of increasing criteria

PATTERN OF PROGRESS	CLICK to mark	REWARD game
1. Build the arousal and chase instincts. Allow the dog to capture the toy.	Capture	More chasing.
2. On first contact with the toy, quickly flick the toy onwards another pace or two. Allow re-capture. As the confidence on first capture builds with a stronger bite, make sure the successful first bites are always rewarded	Responding to recapture	Holding the toy, parading around.
3. Once a consistent grip is achieved, gradually nudge the dog towards you with gentle tugs. Make sure the dog faces you and is guided in by the tug.	Facing you, travelling with good grip.	Parading around with verbal cheering. Release the tension.
4. Drop your hands onto the line and gently bring the dog close to you on the toy.	Facing you and proximity to you.	Parading around with verbal cheering.
5. Once the dog is in position and you are holding the toy on the line, cue the sit. Maintain light tension in the line. If the dog releases prematurely, or slackens the mouth, toss the toy away and expect some chasing before recapture. *	Sitting, whilst holding.	Parading around with verbal cheering.

*Most dogs that are slack or gentle mouthed are also low arousal, ie: they are not likely to become rewarded by the chase game, but by the retrieve sequence. If they are rewarded by chase alone, make sure the premature release ends the game for 20 seconds.

GAME 7:5

Self Control: TUG

Developing:
SELF CONTROL
GOOD MANNERS
UNDERSTANDING
FOCUS

This exercise builds some excellent quality play time with your dog. It also teaches self control, and can be used in small areas. A perfect tool for ensuring focus and developing concentration.

The rules of the game will ensure good manners are maintained.

Tug strength can be developed with different physical exercises and also muscle groups enhanced. (page 90)

PREVIOUS SKILLS
Whippit handling

RESOURCES
Comfortable tug toy for you and the dog.

EXPLORING TUG AND CHASE FUN

PLAY AS FRIENDS: be generous and let the dog win on an equal basis. This game should represent at least 49% winning, (the last win is always yours), as is the offer of the opportunity to play. Do not ask twice.

DUPLICATE THE PREY KILL: this whole game is a practice for real life shredding of fresh kill. The kill can still fight back, either you or the dog want to possess the kill and not share or it can come apart or even run away.

ALWAYS PLAY BY RULES: error bites to your hands, or feet placed against you for increased purchase, end the game.

MIND YOUR BACK: remember to stand up straight when appropriate. If the dog pulls too hard for you, go soft and let go. The harder you pull back the stronger the dog will get. Keep a comfortable grip.

GAME 7:6

Self Control: ON CUE ...

LEVEL 2

Developing:
 STIMULUS CONTROL
 FOCUS
 EXCEPTIONAL
  RESPONSE

PREVIOUS SKILLS

Range of behaviours on
verbal cues

Behaviours that are well established on verbal cues, or even the default behaviour of staying focussed on you, can be taken to an extremely high level through this game.

When play is interspersed with the behaviours, the play time not only rewards the behaviour but the emotions of the game are transferred to the behaviours. The behaviours become more exciting, faster, more focussed, and more desirable.

Response to cue time may be compromised (hesitation) when the excitement, or arousal level, is too high. You will need to adjust the play time to gradually increasing the criteria where the dog shifts from arousal to control. Too much hesitation, take the toy out of sight, refresh the cued behaviour

Experience and plenty of practice can teach a dog to stop in full run after a rabbit .... you just need to build and strengthen the self control muscle.

When teaching a series of behaviours for a performance begin to chain varieties of behaviours. The whole performance will occur between the "give" and the "play" cues.

RESOURCES

Tug toy, or toy on Whippit

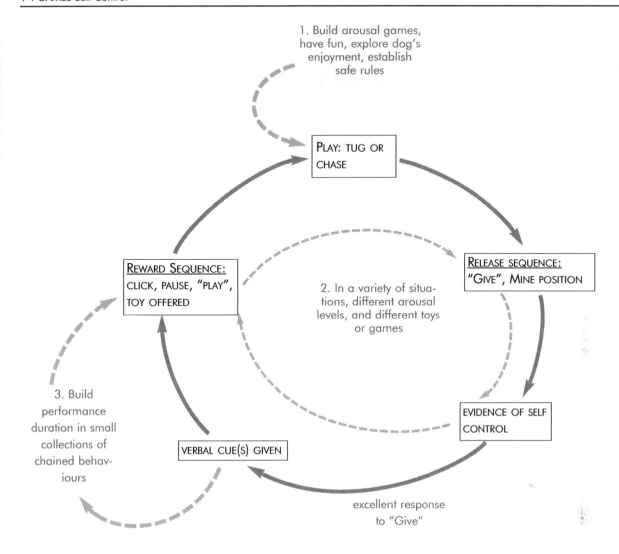

1. Build arousal games, have fun, explore dog's enjoyment, establish safe rules

PLAY: TUG OR CHASE

REWARD SEQUENCE: CLICK, PAUSE, "PLAY", TOY OFFERED

RELEASE SEQUENCE: "GIVE", MINE POSITION

2. In a variety of situations, different arousal levels, and different toys or games

3. Build performance duration in small collections of chained behaviours

EVIDENCE OF SELF CONTROL

VERBAL CUE(S) GIVEN

excellent response to "Give"

MAINTAIN FOCUS

Ensure that the dog does not begin to regard you as the prey rather than the peer.

PATTERN OF PROGRESS Steps of increasing criteria	CLICK to mark	REWARD game
1. Once the dog has a good Give and Take, begin to move around slowly with the toy in your hands. Make sure the dog stays focussed on the toy, not on you.	Focus on toy.	Play
2. Build up speed and animation, make sure the dog watches the toy. Throw the toy ahead and check the chase to the toy is successful.	Continual focus under harder distractions.	Play, or capture and parade.

GAME 7:7   Self Control: FOOLS RUSH IN   LEVEL 3

Developing:
- SELF CONTROL FOR PREY
- IMPULSE CONTROL
- MARK A RETRIEVE

PREVIOUS SKILLS

Quickly flicking the toy on the end of the Whippit.

Self Control Game 7:1.

Give and Take Game 7:2.

Some dogs maintain easily accessible prey instincts. They have not evolved too far from the original model and if left to go wild may possibly survive on their abilities.

The instinctive behaviours will be drawn to the surface through playing tug and chase games.

We can utilise one specific survival kill mechanism and expand it to extremely high levels of self control.

When spotting a rabbit the dog can chase, take a risk of it getting away down a hole or it can stalk in very slowly until close enough to kill before it escapes down the hole. The stalking instinct is still present in many breeds and different types of dogs.

Play the chase games with the Whippit and practice flicking the toy away from the dog as soon as they make any move towards it. Within several repetitions the dog will begin to remain stationary.

RESOURCES

Tug toy on a line, or toy on Whippit.

PATTERN OF PROGRESS Steps of increasing criteria | **CLICK** to mark | **REWARD** location

Pattern of Progress	Click to mark	Reward location
1. Play the chase games with the Whippit and practice flicking the toy away from the dog as soon as they make any move towards it [1].	Any inclination to hesitate or remain stationary.	Flick the toy to the dog to grab[2]

[1]This effectively punishes an approach to the prey.

[2]Do not let the dog run onto the toy after the click, make the toy come onto the dog.

2. Build the strength of the stationary stalking pose with duration, and testing the focus	Stationary pose and focus.	Flick the toy to the dog to grab.
3. Add a cue: This can be the cue to remain stationary when any article is thrown for retrieve, or on approach to stock birds.	Controlled response. Click substituted with cue for behaviour.	Release stationary position with cue for other behaviour: fetch, walk on etc.

8 GAMES Puzzles

This Chapter brings us the "gem" of free shaping. or shaping without minimal guidance.

Very often we have a set plan on what we want to teach the dog and how they are going to learn. Dogs can do so much better than our limited perception of their learning capacity.

Watching a day in the life of a dog, even as an observer, can hint at their true learning potential - and this is everyday dogs, not super dogs, not working dogs, just that dog snoozing over there right now.

- THEY ADAPT from one minute to the next. They look for opportunities to suit their personalities. For the comfort seekers, that patch of sunshine, for the activity freaks the person cutting the grass, for the high appetites, the baby learning to eat. They constantly monitor our routines, learn and anticipate the opportunities close to their desires.

- THEY REMEMBER whole hosts of people, over many months of absence. They can recognise smells of important people over months. They can recognise their siblings, my pups remember me and Amy after years of absence. They recognise our barn for training. They recognise the way you walk in a crowd of people. They recognise the engine sound of your car. They remember the road pattern to their favourite walk. They remember where they last nearly caught a rabbit.

- THEY DISCOVER us as a permanent life long activity. They watch our actions, discover what we like and don't like. They make us laugh, know when we need company and know when we don't. They seem to antici-pate moods, but really they watch our body language, see tension in movement and associate our responses.

- THEY COMPROMISE their life passions to our life style. They can't hunt all day long, but have to enjoy small hunts within their garden. They can't dig and chew and bark and play when it suits them, only when it suits us. They have to wait for us to rise and go to bed, have food at our convenience and learn not to drink from the toilet. They have to learn self control when they would rather be screaming around the light bulb.

The more we discover about dogs the more we should be in awe of them. They moved into our lives and are so integral with us we often take their amazing skills for granted.

They are the BEST learners I have ever had the honour to teach. Anything I assume I will teach the dogs they come up trumps, and show me more than I ever expected.

LETTING THE LEARNER TEACH THE TEACHER

In this section you may well find you are blown away by what your dog can do. Clicker training, and especially free shaping, will open a communication channel that you need to learn to listen to. We bring a range of good teaching skills, but here the learner can teach us what they can do, not what we perceive we want to teach them.

At one of the Clicker Expos in America, Ken Ramirez of the Shedd Aquarium in Chicago, who has oodles of marine mammal training experience, gave a presentation on Modifier Cues. A couple of our trainers were free to attend and gave me a synopsis of the training. Either I wasn't paying proper attention or I translated the process into another filing system. Anyway both versions, Ken's and my mis-adaptation work equally as well, but have different outcomes in the long term life of the cues.

At the next Expo I excitedly reported back to my fellow presenters and was met with a series of "wow, I didn't know dogs could do that". (There seem to be some perception that dolphins could learn this stuff but not dogs, so anything Ken can teach a dolphin I shall make as my personal project to teach the dogs!). My first project was teaching "which is the largest?" All the class plunged in, tried it, and the dogs said, "Yeah cool, what's next".

Huh?

Of course they can tell which is the largest, which is the smallest: which one do you want to kill for dinner? The smallest, slowest? Which one do you not want to fight? The largest, fastest!

CUES FOR PUZZLES

You will need to make a plan for the outcome of the puzzle teaching, especially for modifiers before you begin to teach.

In essence a Modifier cue, is an adverb which describes how any established behaviour is changed, or modified:

The step can be:	backwards	or	forwards
The spin can be	to the left	or	to the right
The paw wave can be:	high	or	low
The go-through can be:	over	or	under

A Modifier cue can be generic and applied to a range of different behaviours that can be modified in the same way:

Left or Right can be:

> Retrieve the article on the left or the article on the right
> Go around the tunnel to the left or to the right
> Wave your front left paw or your front right paw

Fast or Slow can be:

> Come towards me fast or slow
> Carry that object fast or slow
> Go around in a circle fast or slow

The syntax for these cues will be:

> paw left   paw right
> paw left high   paw right low
> retrieve left around right

For competition dogs that need to distinguish the behaviour at speed, there is no time for modifier cues. The dog must know which paw, and what to do with it on the single cue ie:

> paw left = "blue"   paw right = "pink"
> paw left high = "blue up"   paw right low = "pink poorly"
> retrieve left around right = ball, go bye.

The limitation on the cues is constrained by the number of single cues the dog can remember. With modifier cues, combinations of cues will give a greater repertoire, but with slower response time. You will need to choose how you apply your cues, with consideration to your future plans.

PUZZLE SOLVING

To have a sound acquisition on these concepts, and then add appropriate cues, the dog MUST be allowed to learn at their own pace. When they have "got it" you will know. It will take as long as it takes, since the solution requires a thought process, and we have absolutely NO way of telling the dog "think about it".

Even when we play our people teaching games, Genabacab, people have great difficulty thinking laterally. But once the penny drops, and they "get it", they never forget.

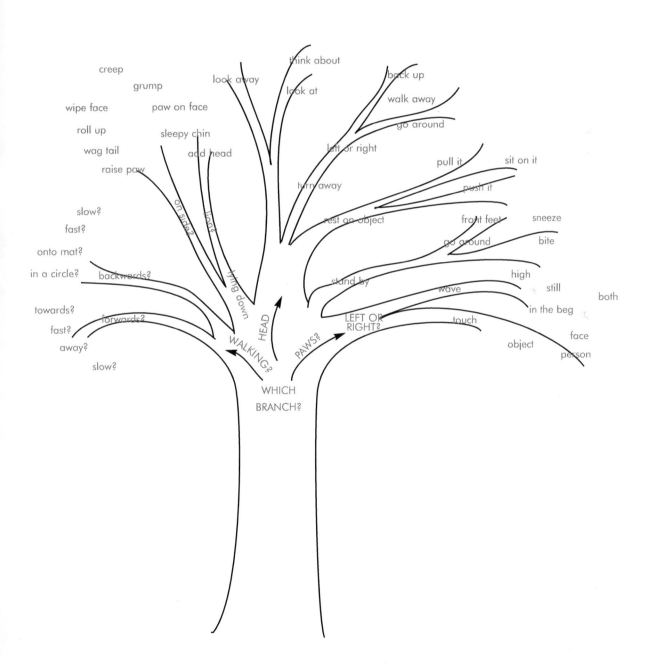

Puzzle solving is a single occurrence thought. Once the solution has arrived, and we celebrate with oodles of repetition, the process is permanently available. Lateral thinking and puzzle solving can be taught, and trained to be more adaptable, more flexible and more creative. But you can never supply it to the learner, only set up situations that give them the opportunity to puzzle out the solutions.

CREATIVE OR DISCIPLINED LEARNING?

When Karen Pryor first published Don't Shoot the Dog in 1986 many folk began their dog's clicker experience with the "101 Things to Do With a Box" exercise. The idea is to place a cardboard box on the floor and click and reward the dog for every new type of interaction with the box: paw touch, nose touch, going around, climbing in, pushing the box etc. Today on my travels I see dogs very experienced in this skill, and so creative. The benefit of this as a learning exercise is to build the confidence of the learner and encourage them to explore their learning, and not wait until they are directed.

Today we have many more experienced clicker teachers, and new generations of pups that are born with learning confidence. Youngsters rarely need the "101 Things with a Box" to develop their skills. The downside of this learning schedule is:

> A learner that never stays with the same behaviour. As soon as the behaviour is rewarded they change the behaviour.
> A really, really cool behaviour can come into the repertoire and be lost as the dog moves onto another behaviour.

But when given a free rein, dogs can find the most amazing behaviours, turn their bodies in unbelievable directions and make us laugh.

Disciplined free shaping will take a dog through their shaping plan on a guided path towards a particular outcome. We can have the benefits of self teaching and develop the skills of puzzle solving at the same time.

I see shaping as a tree. The dog begins at the base of the tree, I sit down in my chair, food and clicker ready: "Aha, we are shaping". The dog then begins to move up the tree and tries the first main branch: Is it my paw? No. They move around the other options. Is it my head? No, Is it my body? Yes. Move it to the left of backwards? etc etc.

The dog with Show Me Something New learning will tend to jump from branch to branch. As soon as the click is withheld, they jump onto a new behaviour rather than explore the possibilities of the existing behaviour: harder, faster, with both paws etc.

LEARNING CAPACITY

Quite simply we don't know what we can yet teach dogs. Demonstrating the largest smallest game will usually bring dog trainers to a stand still. It has deep ramifications: have I underestimated my dog's intelligence all these years? Why didn't I see this before?

Until we have all learned a lot more about what a dog can learn, improved our communication and language skills, and become teacher learners we do not know the capacity of dogs. But it is the MOST exciting time exploring!

For the present I would not advise you overload the dog with too many conceptual puzzles. They are difficult to put on cue, and once the lateral thinking bell has gone off, the dogs seem to be pulled back to the same line of thought. If you start with the Odd One Out, you may not find the Match to Sample as easy as if you had started with it first.

INDICATING BEHAVIOURS

During several of the Puzzle Games your dog will be asked a question:

> Which is the odd one out?
> Which is the smallest?
> Which is mine?
> Where is the drug?

For the dog to be able to communicate their decision to you successfully you will need an indication behaviour. Examples are a paw tap, a paw raise, a down, a fixed look. Avoid using behaviour that would not benefit from being part of the chain, such as retrieve, or walking backwards. If the dog is not correct on their indication, the indicating behaviours can become soured with too many occasions of failure.

To choose an indicating behaviour, place food or the dog's toy in a container that prevents self access. A piece of food in a glass jar, the toy under a brick etc. Set up the situation and reward the dog for trying to get their reward.

Observe which behaviour they are most likely to repeat and mark that to the exclusion of other behaviours. Choosing their natural behaviour in these conditions is more likely to be the least stressful and most obvious behaviour when asked a question.

ENSURE ERRORLESS LEARNING

When teaching a dog to make choice it could be quite easy to take the lazy teaching route and click only when the dog gets it right. If I place 8 objects in front of me and asked the dog "which is the largest" I could wait until the dog touched the correct object and click and reward. But this would also encompass several behaviours that were not correct, ie: the dog indicated on the wrong objects. At the end of a session with 10 questions asked, the dog may error 50 times to 10 correct behaviours. This is an appalling ratio.

On top of this the dog may learn so many things that appear to be what you are looking for but are not right. They may wander around the objects until you click, they may favour the object you have just relocated, they make indicate on the one you most recently handled etc.

The dog needs as much support as they learn as you can give, and your knowledge of your dog and their learning skills will tell you when they seem to be able to anticipate your actions. Keep showing them the solution, and wait until they have made the connection. When they want to anticipate they will show you. (And they soooo enjoy it!)

Teaching puzzles takes team work.

GAME 8:1

PUZZLE: This is a ..?

Developing:
MEMORY SKILLS
MOTOR SKILLS
CAPACITY TO LEARN

PREVIOUS SKILLS
Basic free shaping.
Object interaction.

This game is one of the first we teach young pups. Before they have acquired the skills of adding verbal cues to behaviours, they have the capacity to recognise a large range of objects. They are also developing their motor skills and learning to fine tune them with discipline of repetition.

Pups are perfect free shapers. From around 12 weeks most will have the capacity for this form of learning. Older dogs will also benefit.

Shape approximately 5 behaviours that include:
something with a single front paw for balance and control
something to distinguish left actions from right actions
something for the whole body movement
something that is a geographical location or place to be
a head movement

RESOURCES

5 unique objects that will cue different actions. Choose objects that are easy to distinguish and easy to manipulate: example

small disc	paw left or right
jar lid	paw left or right
plastic bottle	nose touch to cap
small mat	stand on with front feet
cone	go around

TEACHING PLAN Steps of increasing criteria

1. Free shape interaction, either the left front paw or the right front paw with an object. Generalise the object at different heights and angles.

2. Change the object and free shape body movement or nose touch etc. Keep changing object until all behaviours are acquired, and the dog responds when the object is shown without hesitation. This will take several sessions.

3. Place all five objects close to hand, and rotate through the objects. The desired learning is a good response to each object as it is presented, building the number of objects in rotations slowly, starting with two, then three, then four etc.

ADD THE CUE

The object IS the cue, and can be rotated for excellent practise of memory skills.

GAME 8:2

PUZZLE: Where Are You?

LEVEL 3

Developing:
LATERAL THINKING
MIND EXPANSION
CAPACITY TO LEARN

Dogs are quick to acquire new behaviours that are easy for us to teach such as actions, movements etc. But dogs also have a great capacity for knowing where they are, and which way is north, so to speak. They have great geographical awareness. They know where they are relative to other people, dogs and their resources: the den, your back door, the car etc. This capacity can be lost unless exercised.

A challenging teaching exercise

PREVIOUS SKILLS

Go to the mat learning is useful, but not essential

New cue, old cue transition.

RESOURCES

Teaching room with lots of permanent features.

PATTERN OF PROGRESS Steps of increasing criteria	CLICK to mark	REWARD location
1. Place your chair, with your food rewards in the centre of the area. You will always train from this spot. Toss several pieces of food around the room one at a time, and let the dog explore the environment. Note if any one area has a preference, or is favoured, with more desire to collect the food from that area.	Nothing as yet.	With you as the centre of the clock, toss to most points around.
2. Chose a location near a fixed feature, at the edge of your area. When the dog is in that area, click and make double sure the food goes to that area. Throw the food so quickly after the click that the dog cannot leave the area.	The dog in a specific area of the room, where possible different activities.	To the same spot or beyond. Prevent return.
3. Begin to open a gap between the click and the toss, to check that the dog is remaining on the spot when they hear the click.	The dog in a specific area of the room.	To the same spot or beyond. Prevent return.
4. Begin to change the location of the reward to verify that the dog is aware of where they are, and not just staying to where the food lands. You may need to go back to step 2 several times before the dog becomes aware it is their location and not their activity that gets the click.	Proximity to the area.	Around the area, checking the evidence of learning.

ADD THE CUE

Cues for locations can be added at any time, and can be physical area in the room: north, south, east west, or proximity to a piece of furniture: chair, TV, waste bin etc. Work through the new cue old cue protocols.

GAME 8:3 | PUZZLE: Which is this? | LEVEL 3

Developing:
LATERAL THINKING
MIND EXPANSION
CAPACITY TO LEARN

In this game the dog will learn to observe the object you show to them and go find the matching object, and then indicate to you which is the other object in the pair.

Rotate the objects regularly, so that the correct object is not in the same relative position. Make sure when you show the object you want the dog to match that is looks the same from their angle as the one on the floor.

PREVIOUS SKILLS
Basic free shaping.
Change Cue protocol (page 15).

RESOURCES
A range of object (5 - 10) that are in matching pairs. Small enough for you to hold in one hand to show to the dog.

PATTERN OF PROGRESS Steps of increasing criteria   CLICK to mark   REWARD location

NEW CUE / OLD CUE PROTOCOL

Steps	CLICK to mark	REWARD location
1. Begin with the base line behaviour of an indication of equal strength on each object. Take the object one by one, free shape the indicating behaviour. Balance the reinforcement history so that any weak object is brought up to strength. The same behaviour for each object.	Strong indicators on each object when first presented to the dog.	Toss food away to allow you time to swap objects.
2. Place three objects on the floor in a straight line across the front of you. Toss a treat away to 12 o'clock. As the dog returns use your hand to show them which object to indicate on, point or give a hand signal to that object.	Indication behaviour on object you give the signal for.	Toss food out to 12 o'clock. This allows the dog to scan the objects as they return.
3. Once they are happily rotating around the objects, pick up one of the matching pairs, hold it up for the dog to see and then indicate the correct matching object.	Indicating correct object on your cue.	Toss food out to 12 o'clock.

You may need to click the behaviour of observing the object you pick up before they are allowed to go onto the indication.

4. As with New Cue Old Cue transition, keep repeating this sequence until you see the dog disregarding your signal as to which one is correct and anticipating the correct object.	On independent choice of object.	Toss food out to 12 o'clock. Observe the dog's eye movement as they return.

Rotate the objects in the row regularly and introduce new objects, but do not always use the newest object. Remember to check the quality of the indication before introducing new objects. All indications must be equal.

VARIATIONS

Matching by scent can be taught the same way with the New Cue / Old Cue technique.

Using at least 5 identical containers place a very small amount of a substance on a cloth and place in the container (jam jars are good examples). With the dog sitting by your side, ask it to take the scent off a cloth you present to them (you will have 5 matching cloths), and then use your hand to indicate which jar contains the correct matching scent. Always make sure the dog sniffs each jar, you can add a small piece of food to encourage this.

Similar to training scent matching, a person can be picked out by the dog from a sample of their scent. Ask five people to sit in chairs and take five cloths with their hand scent rubbed on the cloths. Remember to write each person's name on the cloths. Ask them to hold their hands on their laps. Give the dog the cloth to sample and then go show the dog which person to indicate on. Gradually wean off your indication until the dog begins to look for the correct person.

FAVOURITE / LEST FAVOURITE

courtesy Ken Ramirez

RESOURCES

A range of toys or objects (10 -15) that vary from their favoured (A) to their least favourite (C) Small enough for you to hold in one hand to show to the dog.

1. Begin by placing each object on the floor between you and the dog one at a time. Reward for the correct indication on each object, and make a note of which you think are the most favoured.		
2. Take an A and C object and hold them behind your back, one in each hand. Show the dog the favourite one, whilst still hiding the other object and make sure they look directly at the object. Return both objects back behind your back, then at the same time place both objects on the floor in front of you.	The dog indicating on their favourite object.	Toss treat away to 12 o'clock
3. Keep working in pairs with the object most likely to be selected as the object you show to the dog. Gradually ask the dog to choose between medium favourite to favourite, then favourite to favourite.	The dog indicating on the object that matches.	Toss treat away to 12 o'clock

Over several sessions:

Choose between Object A and Object C ?	A will be chosen (A is the favourite)
Choose between Object A and Object B ?	A will be chosen (A is the favourite)
Choose between Object B and Object C ?	B will be chosen (B is the favourite)
Choose between Object C and Object B ?	C will be chosen (C is the correct match)
Choose between Object B and Object A ?	B will be chosen (B is the correct match)
Choose between Object C and Object A ?	A will be chosen (C is the correct match)

GAME 8:4

PUZZLE: Odd One Out?

LEVEL 3

Developing:

LATERAL THINKING

MIND EXPANSION

CAPACITY TO LEARN

PREVIOUS SKILLS

Change Cue protocol (page 15).

Indication behaviour: paw tap, look, drop.

This puzzle will follow the New Cue / Old Cue transition process.

The point at which you feel you can remove the old cue is not a precise moment. You will need to observe the body language of the dog. As they return to the objects they will begin to scan the objects, rather than look at your hands, even before they move.

You can gradually withdraw the Old Cue signal, and if the dog is not successful, just keep returning to the Old Cue /New Cue process.

RESOURCES

Four sets of objects that are matching pairs.

PATTERN OF PROGRESS Steps of increasing criteria | CLICK to mark | REWARD location

1. Begin with the base line behaviour of an indication of equal strength on each object. Take the object one by one, free shape the indicating behaviour. Balance the reinforcement history so that any weak object is brought up to strength	Strong indicators on each object when first presented to the dog.	Toss food away to allow you time to swap objects.
2. Placing three objects on the floor between you and the dog. Two are matching pairs, one is the odd one out. Give a hand signal to the odd one out so that the dog can see it as they return from collecting their food.	Indication on object you signal	Toss food out to 12 o'clock. This allows the dog to scan the objects as they return.
3. Rotate the objects so that the Odd One Out changes, and changes location amongst the objects as well. Keep repeating the New Cue (verbal) Old Cue (hand signal) sequence until you feel the dog is ready to try without the signal.	On independent choice of object.	Toss food out to 12 o'clock.

Sample of Object Rotation:

A	A	B		B is correct
A	B	B		A is correct
B	B	C		C is correct
C	B	C		B is correct
A	A	C		C is correct

Once the dog is indicating the odd one from three the number of objects can be increased.

VARIATIONS

The exciting prospect of this learning is the massive potential for making a transition from the odd One Out to the Odd One being the Largest, or Smallest, or furthest away, or different material, etc.

For dogs that have a good acquisition of the odd One Out principal, begin to change the Odd One for consistently the largest one. Make sure you alternate choices, change the largest object, and change the smaller objects.

Once the largest one is errorless, change only one of the other two items. The largest one remains the largest of the three, but it is no longer the odd one out.

ADD THE CUE

Asking Puzzle Questions as cues needs as much help as you can give the dog. Use a verbal question plus a hand signal as the new, New Cue!

GAME 8:5 — PUZZLE: Which is Largest?   LEVEL 3

Developing:
LATERAL THINKING
MIND EXPANSION
CAPACITY TO LEARN

PREVIOUS SKILLS
Basic free shaping
Adding a cue with New cue old cue

Largest by height or by mass? You must decide before you start, as both options are probably observable by the dog.

Do not rush at this. It may take the dog several sessions to grasp the concept. Although we have successfully taught experienced shaping dogs in 10 repetitions. Nah, we didn't believe it either!

RESOURCES

Range of objects of varying height. Examples: cones, stack of bricks, balls. Make sure the height range is no more than slightly above the dog's head to just above floor level.

Use a different series of objects for Smallest.

PATTERN OF PROGRESS Steps of increasing criteria	CLICK to mark	REWARD location
1. Begin with the base line behaviour of an indication of equal strength on each object. Take the objects one by one, free shape the indicating behaviour. Balance the reinforcement history so that any weak object is brought up to strength	Strong indicators on each object when first presented to the dog.	Toss food away to allow you time to swap objects.
2. Placing three objects on the floor between you and the dog. Using the sequence opposite rotate the objects by location and height.	Indication on object you signal	Toss food out to 12 o'clock. This allows the dog to scan the objects as they return.
3. To verify the learning make sure that the object that was once successful is now NOT the largest, but is still present.	On independent choice of object.	Toss food out to 12 o'clock.

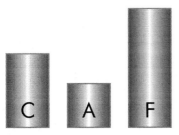

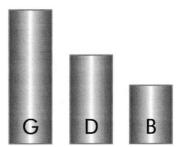

1. Rotate which is the largest object, and the location of the largest object

2. "G" is the largest object.

3. "F" was not the largest object and was correctly rejected, it now becomes the successful largest object.

ADD THE CUE

Asking Puzzle Questions as cues needs as much help as you can give the dog. Use a verbal question plus a hand signal as the new, New Cue!

GAME 8:6   **PUZZLE: Something New?**   **LEVEL 3**

Developing:
  LATERAL THINKING
  MIND EXPANSION
  CAPACITY TO LEARN

PREVIOUS SKILLS
Basic free shaping

The cue for "show me something new" will be a shaping rug. This needs to be large enough for the dog to work on and maintain their position. A hearth rug would be ideal.

If the dog is free shaping on the rug, the default is "something new". When something new comes along that you wish to work with or keep, then remove the rug and the dog should stay with the same behaviour.

To establish the rug as the cue for "something new", begin with a range of several objects to hand. For each behaviour swap the object and click when the behaviour offered is different, as well as a different object. A paw tap with subsequent objects is too similar.

Remove the rug and stay with the same object, rewarding repetitions of the same behaviour 5 times.

Replace the rug and move onto new objects.

RESOURCES
Shaping Rug, range of 10 new objects to interact with.

PATTERN OF PROGRESS Steps of increasing criteria	CLICK to mark	REWARD location
1. Place rug on floor with Object A.	A behaviour.	On the rug.
2. Change to Object B.	A new behaviour.	On the rug.
3. Change to Object C.	A new behaviour.	On the rug.
4. Change to Object D.	A new behaviour.	On the rug.
5. Change to Object E.	A new behaviour.	On the rug.
6. Remove the rug. Place Object E on floor. Repeat 5 times.	The same behaviour.	On the floor.
7. Place rug on floor with Object , then G, then H etc.	New behaviours.	On the rug.
8. Keep rotating between 6 and 7 looking for the dog anticipating the cue to repeat or look for something new.	As the rug indicates.	On the rug or floor.

VARIATIONS

Once the dog has established the rug and the cue for something new, extend the creativity by:

Something new, no object at all

Same Object but do something new with this object

Whole bunch of objects on the rug, change object each time

From this we can look for exciting new behaviours that the dog has created and probably enjoys. These can be interactions with objects or stand alone movements.

Additionally with the "change object" behaviour we can teach a repetition of the same behaviour, but changing objects such as :

Put your toys away   ie: go fetch a new toy each time

Ring the bells   ie: touch a different bell each time

ADD THE CUE

Let the rug be the cue for "Something New", and:

the presence of a single object on the rug	=	something new with this object
no objects on the rug	=	anything new you can do on the rug
several objects on the rug	=	same behaviour, new object each time

so which is the largest?

GLOSSARY

Adding a cue — The process of putting a behaviour under stimulus control. Usually a word, signal, activity, environment or object. Step by step progress is detailed in the Clicker Trainers Series: Foundation Book by Kay Laurence.

Aerobic exercise — Develops and maintains cardiovascular fitness: strengthening the heart, improve the capacity of the lungs and controls weight.

Anaerobic exercise — Focuses on specific muscles and their size, endurance, and strength. Weight lifting and resistance training are examples of human anaerobic exercise.

Default behaviour — The behaviour the dog should adapt when they hear no cue, or they cannot remember the given cue.

Flexigility — An exercise programme designed to build balance, experience and flexibility

Flick Click — Flicking movement of hand that indicates the behaviour that earns the reward. It may end with a tossed treat, or just be a movement to the food reserve.

Free shaping — Where the learner chooses their path of progress towards the teacher's goal. Free from cues, prompts or lures.

Learning Gap — The area between what is already achieved and the goal we aim for

Micro shaping — Teaching by micro steps, errorless free shaping with accuracy and 95% success rate. see Clicker Trainers Series: Intermediate

Modifier Cue — Where the behaviour is "modified" by a preceding cue: faster slower, left or right, higher or lower.

Neural pathways — Connections in the brain between different parts, can combine functions. These are established during brain development, and utilised through the dog's life.

Reinforcer — Something that makes the behaviour stronger. This is not always a deliverable reward, but can be your animation or response to the dog's behaviour.

Rewards — Anything the learner perceives as rewarding at that time. Usually food, toys, attention activity etc.

Rewards for outcomes or actions. The teacher plans whether the learning is the process or the final outcome. When learning to drive a car, the process of driving is the key learning, not arriving at a fixed venue.

Self control — Where the dog exhibits control over impulse reactions.

Target stick — Stick that a target object is attached to. Usually hand held and used to create direction and movement.

Targeting — Learning through another behaviour. Using objects to cue certain actions that give guidance to the next stage of learning. See also Chapter 3 Games with Objects

Visual Click — Hand movement indicating the behaviour that earns the reward, such as offering the reward.

Whippit — Toy fixed to the end of whip, lunge whip or driving whip.

INDEX

41091329R00095

Made in the USA
Lexington, KY
01 May 2015